Rethinking Development:
Perspectives from
the Caribbean and Atlantic Canada

Rethinking Development: Perspectives from the Caribbean and Atlantic Canada

*Proceedings of an International Conference
at Saint Mary's University
Halifax, Nova Scotia
October 25-28, 1984*

edited by Henry Veltmeyer

International Education Centre
Issues in International Development Series, No. 1

International Education Centre
Issues in International Development Series

1. *Rethinking Development: Perspectives from the Caribbean and Atlantic Canada*, edited by Henry Veltmeyer

2. *Rethinking Caribbean Development*, edited by George Schuyler and Henry Veltmeyer

The International Education Centre seeks to educate Canadians about international development and multicultural issues in order to increase public awareness, strengthen social justice and encourage the emergence of informed and responsible citizens of the world community.

Proceedings of a conference sponsored by the Canadian International Development Agency and the Social Sciences and Humanities Research Council of Canada.

Typesetting and Design by *LaserGraphics* in Halifax, Nova Scotia
Cover Design by Ken Wallace

Canadian Cataloguing in Publication Data

Main entry under title:

Rethinking development

(Issues in international development; 1)
"Proceedings of an international conference at Saint Mary's University, Halifax, Nova Scotia, October 25-28, 1984."
ISBN 0-921793-00-6

1. Atlantic Provinces - Economic policy - Congresses.
2. Caribbean Area - Economic policy - Congresses.
3. Atlantic Provinces - Social policy - Congresses.
4. Caribbean Area - Social policy - Congresses.
I. Veltmeyer, Henry. II. Saint Mary's University (Halifax, N.S.).
International Education Centre.

HC117.A7R48 1987   338.9715   C87-094434-7

Contents

Keynote Addresses

Workshop Sessions

Summation Address

Concluding Sessions

Appendices

Acknowledgments

Publication of these proceedings, and the conference itself, were financed by generous grants from the Canadian International Development Agency (Public Participation Branch) and the Social Sciences and Humanities Research Council of Canada. These financial contributions are gratefully acknowledged, as neither the conference nor its various outcomes, which include a considerable array of intellectual exchanges, would have been possible without them.

In addition, we are grateful to the Government of Nova Scotia (the Department of Development), the Council of Maritime Premiers, the Atlantic Provinces Economic Council and various other organizations and community groups (see Appendix 1) that provided valuable organizational or financial support.

We are also grateful to Anthony Bryan, Director of the Institute of International Relations at Saint Mary's University, for his help in designing and organizing the conference; and to Saint Mary's University itself, with particular regard to the valuable secretarial assistance provided by members of the Word-processing Centre. As for the final copy editing of the entire proceedings, attention should be drawn to the exceptional professional work of Douglas Beall, who has managed to extract a measure of order out of relative chaos.

Preface

This volume contains the proceedings of a conference entitled "Rethinking Development in the 1980s", held in October 1984 at Saint Mary's University, Halifax, Nova Scotia, and co-sponsored by that university's International Education Centre and the Institute of International Relations of the University of the West Indies at St. Augustine, Trinidad.

Some 52 presentations were made at the conference, including five major addresses, eight presentations at two plenary sessions, and 38 presentations in the context of 20 workshops. Although Michael Manley, former Prime Minister and Leader of the Opposition in Jamaica, attracted an audience of over 1,100, the three-day conference sustained the participation of 200-250 registered participants in addition to the 25 invited speakers from the Caribbean, a corresponding number of Canadian speakers, and 30 or so persons in some officiating capacity. The strong interest generated by the conference arose out of the importance of its central theme, the internationally comparative focus of its presentations and discussions, and the exceptional scope and quality of these exchanges.

The aim of the conference was to contribute ideas towards a solution of the prevailing crisis in theory and policy relative to the social and economic development of those regions and countries that find themselves on the periphery of an increasingly global economic order. The sources of this intellectual and political crisis are unclear, but they undoubtedly reflect conditions of the economic crisis that has gripped much of the Western world since the early 1970s. Although the sources of this economic crisis are also unclear, it seems possible to assert that: (1) the position a country or region occupies in this global order is a crucial determinant of the level and form of its economic development; and (2) the process of economic development is systematically uneven, with peripheral countries and regions subject to forces that tend to inhibit their development and to promote conditions of their underdevelopment.

This issue has thrown the entire field of development into disarray, leading to the observed crisis in theory and policy—and economic reality. The conference on rethinking development was organized in Halifax, the major metropolitan centre of a region with a long experience of economic underdevelopment, as one response to this crisis.

On the conference program were academics and representatives from the public and private sectors of two regional communities—the Caribbean and Atlantic Canada—with considerable experience and a specialist interest in questions of national and regional development. A major objective of the conference was to create a forum for a comparison of (1) the conditions of development and underdevelopment problems and (2) the history of responses to them, both at the level of public policy and in the civil societies of the respective regions. There were several reasons for this comparative format. For one thing, the countries in the Caribbean basin and the provinces of Atlantic Canada share elements of a history that can be traced back several centuries (to a mercantilist trade in rum and codfish). For another, both regions are similarly located in the Western economic system based on the accumulation of capital on a global scale—to use a phrase coined by Samir Amin, an economist with the United Nations and a notable exponent of a "world systems" theory of economic development.

Because of the similarity in the experiences of people in the two regions, and a common concern with conditions of underdevelopment and development, it was felt that a conference bringing together specialists from both of these parts of the world could make a substantial contribution to the process of rethinking development in the two regions and beyond. The following edited proceedings show that the conference did indeed make such a contribution. It is hoped that the lessons which could be (and were) drawn by the several hundred participants will contribute to the process of rethinking the conditions of and prospects for national and regional development and have some impact on public policy in Canada and the Caribbean.

Unfortunately, because of various technical problems in tape recording and transcribing some workshop sessions, the proceedings are incomplete. Presentations and discussions in several workshops (see the program listed in Appendix 2) could not be or were not transcribed or summarized. Most of the proceedings, however, are made available in this volume either as edited transcripts of major addresses and remarks or as summaries provided by session chairpersons, various recorders or by myself, the person responsible for organizing the conference and editing these proceedings.

Also, a number of presentations were based on prepared papers that will be available in two volumes to be published separately. Papers related to development issues in the Caribbean appear in the book, *Rethinking Caribbean Development*, published by the International Centre at Saint Mary's University, and papers related to Atlantic Canadian development issues will appear in a separate volume to be published by the Gorsebrook Research Institute of Atlantic Canada Studies at Saint Mary's.

Henry Veltmeyer

Opening Addresses

Robert Moore: *From the 1960s to the 1980s*

(Robert Moore is a past high commissioner of Guyana to Canada)

Ladies and gentlemen, I will keep my remarks brief. When the 1960s began, a major revolution had just taken place in Cuba, the implications of which were waiting to be digested by the Caribbean, and a major institution of the Commonwealth Caribbean, the Federation of the West Indies, was doomed to be dismantled.   When the 1980s began, a major Caribbean institution had recently been established in Grenada, the implications of which the rest of the Caribbean was uncomfortably digesting.

The period from the 1960s to the 1980s was a period of search for Caribbean people, and part of that search constitutes the nature of this conference. What were the primary searches of Caribbean people? One was the search for viability—economic and fiscal. A second was the search to discover what independence really meant if there was already independence, or what it would mean if there was not.

After the dismemberment of the West Indies federation, some Caribbean countries were searching for a viable economy of their own, an economy which would generate wealth, in some cases by the exploitation of their own natural resources, in other cases by the begging bowl. Some Caribbean temperments felt the "dependency syndrome" was the optimum condition—that to beg was *to be*, and to beg eloquently was *to be fully*—and, therefore, dependency was not in any way a blot but the natural condition of small Caribbean countries. To be dependent was to be realistic.

Other Caribbean countries felt that the "dependency syndrome" was merely a latter-day extension of the colonialist mentality, that imperialism would merely become neo-imperialism if Caribbean countries went on being dependent. These countries searched for self-reliance. They wanted to know what *developmen—* at that time a mysterious word—meant and what sort of development should be attempted. What they slowly came to discover was that independence is a synonym for aloneness—when a country becomes independent, it becomes alone. Therefore, the big question of their existence and of their external relationships was: What do we do with this aloneness? How do we mitigate the aloneness of a sovereign state in an international system that is becoming increasingly abrasive? Do we exchange the Pax Britannica for the Pax Americana? In short, do we move from being a colony to being a client? If we will have neither the Pax Britannica that went with the departure of empire nor the Pax Americana, can we create a regional relationship and consciousness expressed in regional institutions which we could call a "Pax Caribbean?" This has been one of the most enduring searches of Caribbean people from the 1960s to now.

Another major search of Caribbean people has been to turn the game of independence into benefits for the broad masses of people who still live at the bottom of society. The West Indies began its federation fearing the effects of the Cuban revolution on the Caribbean, fearing that this curious thing called communism would make inroads into their liberal values and erode them. Revolution, many said, was not the West Indian way. To overthrow a regime by violent means is distinctly Latin and, after all, we are inheritors of the English way of tempering injustice by pressure until injustice becomes a shadow, the pressure becomes a reality, and then finally the reality becomes an institution. Therefore, many West Indians take the term *revolution* to mean a restructuring of society in the direction of greater accountability to the broad masses of people, without the connotation of convulsions like those implied by the Cuban revolution.

This raised the question of what format the Commonwealth Caribbean states would have. Was the Westminster system—two houses of parliament, elections every four or five years—relevant to the Caribbean? Was a written constitution relevant to these small territories? Could you work a parliamentary system with another reality largely imitated from the textbooks of North America, the "trickle down" theory of development? As votes trickled up to parliament, so it was assumed that the pressure of the people's representatives would cause the wealth generated by local corporations, multinational corporations, government bureaucrats and the local elite to trickle down—a seesaw effect. As political pressures from below went up, so wealth would come down. The search for this combination of political trickle-up and economic trickle-down became one of the enduring searches of the Caribbean.

That search led in the 1970s to considerable criticism of the whole system by those who began to see in the West Indies not so much a dialectic of unequal relationships between wealth and non-wealth as a dialectic between those who were Black and poor and those who were Black and non-poor. So, in the 1970s, Black consciousness of one sort or another grew in the Caribbean to attempt to answer the whole economic and constitutional problem in a different way. The people at the bottom, it was said, are largely Black people (in Guyana, Black and Indian). Development must begin with them and it must spiral up, which means that the control of government must be exercised by mechanisms not entirely patterned on the Westminster model.

The Grenadian revolution, that coup de radio that drove the old man out of the country and instituted a fascinating group of bright young people, attempted to play the city-state democracy ideal in the Caribbean, the ideal that Eric Williams had preached in his university of Woodford Square but apparently forgot when he achieved the prime ministership of his country. Many West Indians were mesmerized, wanting to see whether the Grenada experiment would work and to find out what it would mean for the

Westminster parliamentary system, whether the experiment would have to go or whether it would be tolerated by other West Indians. In short, a third great search in the Caribbean was the search for a plurality of systems within an economic community that had been founded in the early 1970s.

All of these searches continue. Today, we are observing the anniversary of the presence of foreign troops in Grenada. That itself shows you how dynamic and far-reaching these searches have been. It also tells you that West Indians are now divided between, on one side, a philosophy of plurality in the Caribbean within a framework that is not federal but communal and, on the other side, a feeling that the West Indies must be monochrome in its political philosophy.

The West Indies are a laboratory for the Third World. Many of the fundamental issues that other Third World countries are discussing have been agitated, thought about, quarrelled about and written about in the West Indies. That is why it is extremely important for Canadians to look critically and thoughtfully at the Caribbean, for they will learn a great deal from these laboratory mini-societies about most of the fundamental questions of our era and the way different people meet these questions. They will learn a lot about alternative philosophies of development and alternative concepts of evolution, devolution and revolution.

Dale Bisnauth: *Canada and the Caribbean: Re-examining an Important Relationship*

(Rev. Dale Bisnauth is with the Caribbean Council of Churches and the Ecumenical Council of Canada)

This part of Canada and the Caribbean share more than ready access to the Atlantic. The ties that bind us—economic, social and political—go back to those early days when the Caribbean and Canada were being explored and exploited for the benefit of outside interests. In those days the Caribbean was regarded by European powers as of much greater importance than Canada. When the whole Caribbean came to be regarded as one vast sugar plantation, a European hinterland to be developed by non-European, slave-intensive labour, Atlantic Canada served as a source of cheap food—codfish—

for these labourers and as a small market for the rum and molasses that that labour produced, and provided the hogsheads in which Caribbean sugar was shipped to Europe.

I am a Presbyterian. The Presbyterian Church in Guyana will celebrate its 100th birthday next year. That particular church began as a mission of the Canadian Presbyterian Church, and many of the missionaries who went to Guyana and Trinidad went on those codfish boats from Atlantic Canada.

Times have changed, and things have changed dramatically and for the better for Atlantic Canada but slowly, agonizingly and not appreciably for the better for the Caribbean. Nothing demonstrates this perceived and real difference better than the fact that you, in these parts, locate us in the Third World. Some people even describe the Caribbean as the Third World's third world.

By the 1960s, as Robert Moore has indicated, political change was coming to Caribbean countries in the form of independence from Britain. That power was well on the road to dismantling its empire. Political independence held a possibility for new nations to determine their several destinies and to develop in ways that were in keeping with their resources and potential, however they might choose to do so, but vision has a way of painfully colliding against harsh reality.

The fact of the matter is that political independence has led to little more than the frustration of people's expectations. Such has been the frustration over our lack of real development in the Caribbean that not a few people, who should know better, yearn for what they consider "the good old days of colonialism." Others, giving up on the region, have sought the lotusland elsewhere, not least of all in Canada, and this has led to a "brain drain" that continues to impoverish our part of the world.

The causes of our underdevelopment or undevelopment are too well known and too well analysed to be heard one more time. Suffice it to say that the causes of our underdevelopment are infinitely more profound and deep-rooted than those usually itemized by people in developed countries. The causes are rooted in the harsh realities of our history (slavery, indentureship, colonialism); in geopolitical realities (we happen to be located next door to the United States of America); in the inequities of an unjust economic world-order, the continued economic plunder of an already repeatedly raped region by conglomerates that have their base in the developed world; and in the insensitivity, to the point of deaf arrogance, of the powerful to the needs of poor nations to come to maturity in ways that dignify them and lead to national cohesiveness and integrity. I would not want to leave you with the impression that we in the Caribbean are not painfully aware that there are factors local to us that inhere in our social, economic, political and cultural structures that are also responsible for our continued impoverishment.

What has been Canada's role in our development or underdevelopment from the 1960s to the present time? The single most important tool of Canada's foreign policy towards the Third World in general and towards the Caribbean in particular has been foreign aid. The claim has been made that Canada's largesse has won her international respect as a rich nation committed to Third World development. I would not want to dispute this reputation, but I must insist that the reality is that, whatever the volume of Canadian aid to Third World countries, those countries remain as poor, exploited and oppressed as they were three decades ago.

An assumption regarding development has been excluded. It was assumed that all that Third World countries needed to achieve development was an input of the resources, capital and technical know-how that they lacked. However, Third World countries have been saying since, if not before, the 1960s that what is needed for development is not aid but justice. Not a band-aid approach that can at best only prolong the miserable life of ailing economies but a kind of radical surgery that would lead to a new international economic order. The voices of Caribbean columnists, politicians, novelists, historians and church spokespersons all rose in the 1960s to make the point that to merely reform the structure and flow of foreign aid, whatever the secondary importance of that aid, was not enough. The most urgent, primary task was and still is the restructuring of North-South economics and trade relations.

In the 1970s the Canadian International Development Agency (CIDA) came under heavy flak in Canada for not doing the job of developing the poor nations properly because of bureaucratic incompetence. This incompetence was advanced as the main cause for the failure of aid to engender development.

A Canadian stereotype of those who refuse to develop was encapsulated in a *Toronto Sun* comment that, "Some races or nationalities seem to have an inclination and talent for business enterprise and hard work, others do not." Underdevelopment in the Caribbean in the late 19th century was, in the opinion of people like Englishman Thomas Carlyle, the result of the indolence of people who lived with pumpkins up to their ears and therefore had no incentive to be enterprising. Crude, but only a bit more so than the *Sun*'s attempt to account for the failure of aid to advance Third World development.

The sharp criticism of Canadian aid programs made it difficult at first to understand why in 1980 the External Affairs Minister committed Canada to increasing its aid to the international standard of 0.7 percent of Canada's gross national product by 1990. That commitment came in spite of the recognition that aid made no appreciable contribution to the economic growth of Third World countries, some 90 of which were recipients of Canadian charity. It came in spite of the recognition that aid was often inefficiently allocated and, more important still, that there had been no appreciable reduction in disparities of income between rich and poor nations and within poor nations themselves.

A search for motives behind the 1980 commitment will reveal what has not always been articulated publicly, that Canada's development policy vis-à-vis Third World countries has always been politically motivated. Remember the 1980 Brandt Commission report (*North-South: A programme for survival*) on this matter. The commission asked for a massive transfer of resources to the Third World to avoid widespread starvation and poverty, and warned that if a program for survival was not implemented quickly, the world could face international conflict with global annihilation. I wish to suggest that it was this report more than anything that elicited the 1980 commitment.

The political motive was always there. It launched the Colombo Plan in the 1960s. Was it not Lester B. Pearson who said in 1950, "Communist expansion may well spill over into Southeast Asia as well as into the Middle East. If Southeast and South Asia are not to become conquered by communism, we of the free democratic world must demonstrate that it is we, and not the Russians, who stand for national liberation and economic and social progress"? Is it not true that when Britain was reluctant, while dismantling its empire in the Caribbean, to leave its first world colonies undefended against possible socialist influence from within or outside the region, that Canada agreed to be the insurance against this with its Commonwealth Caribbean Assistance Program in 1958? John Diefenbaker once said, "Fifty million dollars a year would be cheap insurance for Canada to halt communism in Asia." I have no indication as to how he computed the cost of that insurance in relation to the Caribbean. In the late 1960s, when anti-communist arguments began to wear thin, the philanthropic motive was raised. As late as 1969, CIDA was saying that its first objective was "to establish within the recipient countries military alliances or bases that will assist Canada or Canada's Western allies to maintain a reasonably stable and secure international political system," and this was after 1968, when Pierre Trudeau's government had the External Aid Office restructured into the Canadian International Development Agency. You will note that the word "Aid" was omitted.

Throughout the 1970s, government spokespersons de-emphasized the political aims behind the aid. The rhetoric was that Canada had no political ambition in the developing world. We are still not convinced of this in the Caribbean.

In this world, it is too much to ask any government or nation to act in relation to others without some political motivation. It is unrealistic to expect that nations would not be motivated by political concerns. Churches are motivated by political concerns. I wish to suggest that there is no theological posture, no style of being religious, of being Christian, that does not have written into it an ideology of power. That ideology may not be articulated but it is nevertheless there. If that can be true of the Church, however much we Church people may like to say that that is not true, should we expect governments to act in relation to other governments and peoples without political motivations? One would hope that that motivation would be enlightened and in the best interests of all concerned, but in the Caribbean, an ideologically plural region as Robert Moore has indicated, Canada's approach to development from a particular ideological position can be destructive and destabilizing. Within nations that are politically plural, that approach can have painful consequences for internal politics, not because of that approach as such—because Canadian aid is still small—but because Canada seems so dependent on Washington, our powerful neighbour to the north. When we know that one of the formulators of CIDA's policy admitted, "We are no more independent in our aid policy than we are in our defence of foreign countries," we have cause to look a gift horse in the mouth.

What are we to make of the exceptional grant of $298,000 in food aid to the Dominican Republic in 1966? Was it part of the clean-up campaign of the U.S. invasion of that country in 1965? Does CIDA continue to operate in Grenada in 1984, and in what ways? The fact that Canada has consistently supported U.S. positions in negotiations over the new international economic order, what are we to make of that?

During this conference we'll have time to ponder those questions. The stated objectives of most agencies may be philanthropic, but we note those philanthropic motives for what they are worth. We know that Canada is also the beneficiary of its own aid programs. For example, there is a direct linkage between food aid and agricultural programs in Canada. The airports and water systems in the Caribbean are more beneficial to the tourist industry, which depends on outside imports, than to Caribbean nations. When the real cost of aid is computed it can be demonstrated that it is not as costly to Canada as it is sometimes made out to be; it may even be beneficial. A 1983 CIDA statement said: "Sixty percent of our total aid budget is spent in Canada for goods and services provided to developing countries." The sum is close to $650 million annually. "It is estimated that over 100,000 jobs can be related to [Canadian] foreign aid programs. The bilateral aid programs provide foreign markets for key Canadian industries and they sometimes represent a major source of contracts." Where shall we put the problems caused by the introduction of inappropriate technologies, projects developed in economic and social conditions different from those in the Caribbean? What about the ravages done to our economies by Canadian multinationals?

I must not go on in this vein lest I give the impression that Canada (and particularly the Atlantic Provinces) and the Caribbean can never be engaged in a developmental process that could benefit us mutually, with probably the greater benefits accruing to the Caribbean, which has been so sinned against in the past, even though people have tried to be charitable to us in their own way.

Although Canada pursued these programs through the decades, guided by the policies I have tried to adumbrate, the Caribbean in the 1980s still remains terribly underdeveloped despite some illusion of development here and there, a few token successful projects. Economically, we are heavily indebted and some of us are at the mercy of the International Monetary Fund (IMF), the World Bank and other lending agencies that seek to make us pursue their agendas to underdevelopment. Politically, we remain caught in vicious, internecine, interparty strife that leaves us as nations with neither the energy nor direction for development. Socially, we are still fragmented societies with a vision of a new Caribbean and of new Caribbean men and women. The malaise and viciousness that followed the events in Grenada on October 25th, 1983, evidences our impotence to deal effectively with problems related to our geopolitics, problems exacerbated by America's neurotic anxiety to regard Cuba as a surrogate of the USSR in the Caribbean and a base for the spread of communism in the region. This neurosis is primarily responsible for the way the USA tailors its aid to Caribbean states.

What is Canada's position in all of this? I wish to suggest that beyond 1984 there must be a new approach to Canada's contribution toward development. The sole purpose for aid-giving can only be to assist the Caribbean countries and people in their struggle towards integral development and self-reliance. That would mean that you cannot see your programs and policies as primarily directed towards boosting Canadian export and investment. If you are thinking in terms of subsidizing private companies that want to invest in the Caribbean, we would suggest that you think again. Priority should be given to the support of local, low-cost projects where financial aid is spent on the purchase of local goods and services obtained in the region. If you are serious about Caribbean development, then the political component that has always influenced Canadian gift-giving must be radicalized. National and multilateral aid programs would have be to severed from the imperial strategies of the powerful north.

A criteria for selecting development partners should be the partners' commitment to authentic, all-around development with a special bias to the poor, the marginalized and the powerless in our part of the world. Development assistance should be withheld from any Caribbean country that maintains gross social inequalities and pursues a path that denies, in some cases, the majority of people their fundamental human rights. It may mean targeting aid to those areas and people where the aid can help to correct injustices and to empower people rather than to increase the might of elitist regimes.

All of this means we should move together—Canada and the Caribbean, and all donors and recipients in the North-South relation—from an attitude of patronage and opportunism to a new stance of solidarity. Living in solidarity demands that we place the blame for underdevelopment where it belongs: on the elite classes, governments and corporations that create and perpetuate unjust international structures which oppress and dehumanize the majority of the people for the enrichment of the few. Together, in solidarity, we must begin the process that will result in the liberation of all the people in the Caribbean and Atlantic Canada from conditions that make it difficult for us to create just, humane, sustainable societies of free persons responsible for charting their own courses towards development.

Plenary Sessions

DEVELOPMENT MODELS AND THEORIES: AN ASSESSMENT

Summary of Presentations

by Peter MacLellan

Kari Levitt (Centre for Developing Area Studies, McGill University, Montreal; transcript follows) began by asking conference participants to remember that "book learning" is no substitute for learning from experience, making specific reference to Grenada to illustrate this point. Learning from experience can be painful and disillusioning, and requires a certain resiliency. Grenada was a setback for progressive forces in the region, but it represented a certain reality and any study that ignores such experiences is useless. Many academic efforts have failed because they blindly attempt to impose theory on reality.

The two regions being examined during the conference share some of the characteristics of peripheral capitalism, and the Atlantic region particularly illustrates the concept of polarization within an economic union. However, some significant differences must be remembered. For example, the free movement within the region and the presence of equalization payments place Atlantic Canada in a more favoured position than the Caribbean.

The Caribbean must live with the fact that the United States considers it to be in its own "backyard." A case in point is the success of the USA in cutting short the Grenada experiment.

It is of paramount importance to formulate new development models that recognize the realities of the 1980s.

Another point Levitt made had to do with the so-called "debt problem,"' a problem that has resulted in a massive drain of capital from Latin America to the world's banks ($50 billion in just two years) and brutal problems facing the ordinary people of the region, who never benefitted from the original loans.

Levitt reminded the audience that although the recession did not cripple the industrialized countries, it has been a disaster for the Caribbean. The crisis means we must free ourselves from the rhetoric of contending ideologies and rethink all theories of "economic determinism" from both the right and the left of the political spectrum. She called for an open-minded approach to the entire problem of development.

Any discussion of development models must not get bogged down in dogma because models can be transitory and "faddish." Levitt expressed no preference for any particular development model because she wished to avoid slavish dogmatism.

She maintained that any approach must cultivate a sense of history and the knowledge that all models are not universally transferable; one must always consider the factors of culture and ethnicity.

Recognizing that there is a crisis, she believed the proper approach was one unburdened by any specific ideology. One must recognize the reality of world capitalism and understand how it works and is protected. As a system, it promotes international economic relations over national sovereignty and tends to keep a tight leash on Third World countries. Economics reflects power relationships.

In closing her remarks, Levitt made reference to economist Sir Arthur Lewis in stating that liberation has to be a triumph of politics over economics.

James Sacouman (Sociology, Acadia University, Wolfville, Nova Scotia) stated that the conference really dealt with two kinds of regions—(1) a region within an existing state and (2) a multinational region within the world—but that both regions represented "peripheralization." Sacouman differed from Levitt's approach to the theme by giving a Marxist critique of development models and by stressing that models are essential and that theory and ideology are the bulwark of model-building.

He alluded to current "mainstream" theories, which attribute underdevelopment in the region to either (1) a lack of resources, (2) the wrong mix of resources, (3) cultural backwardness or (4) incompetent politicians, as being unable to articulate the regions' requirements.

Sacouman reminded the audience that capitalism requires labour that is cheap, mobile and tractable. He stated that there are problems with Marxist theories, making special reference to the belief that regional underdevelopment reflects insufficient capitalist development and that conditions for socialism have to develop elsewhere—at the centre of capitalist development—before they can occur in a region such as Atlantic Canada.

He advanced the idea that capitalism needs to produce uneven development for "zooification." It needs regions that will produce people who can live cheaply and whose labour is cheap. This idea is derived from Marx's theory of surplus labour pools. Referring to this theory, Sacouman spoke of a process of semiproletarianization in Atlantic Canada, where many workers entertain the conceit of semi-independence by doing a bit of farming, fishing, lumbering and so on, but actually never achieve full-time employment and are forced to accept successive layoffs as part of life. This labour pool, or "labour zoo," has been historically essential to the development of capitalism in Central Canada.

The solution for Atlantic Canada, according to Sacouman, rests in two realities: (1) the small producers are the only ones who have made real progress towards development and (2) these efforts almost always have been blocked by larger interests.

He listed the global options for development as: (1) the continued evolution of capitalism; (2) statism (the Soviet model), where a state elite lives off the collective wealth; (3) global extermination as a result of the conflict between the first two options; or (4) socialism, the only model that will allow true development, which requires true worker and community control.

Sacouman said that we must clearly examine historical class alliances and understand why they have failed. We must link present class and gender struggles, using strategies that exclude capitalist and statist models.

He concluded by saying, "the only theory of development that counts is the theory that puts power in the hands of the people."

Cheddi Jagan, the former prime minister of Guyana, began (transcript follows) by stating that we must put things into perspective when discussing models and options. The capitalist world-powers have consistently opposed and helped to destroy "communist" development models in the Caribbean. We should challenge the capitalist system.

He discussed the Soviet liberation of Eastern Europe and the Western reaction led by Churchill and Truman against the subsequent spread of communism. This reaction included a call for world capitalism and led to a situation in which the United States assumed the mantle of world imperialism after World War II. The Truman Doctrine pledged to halt revolutionary movements, a position still reflected in the current U.S. approach to Central America. The same approach was evident in the reaction of the United States against his own government in Guyana during the 1960s and subsequently against governments in Chile and Jamaica, to name a few.

The Truman Doctrine, Jagan maintained, was dedicated to the export of world capitalism and to the creation of Third World dependency. The model advocated created an investment climate to attract capital, particularly into tax-free situations, and the result was an eventual outflow of regional capital.

The current Latin American debt problem illustrates the result of capitalist theory according to Jagan. The imperialists' job is to plunder, to sow one dollar and reap four.

A system has been established where the countries continue to borrow and the workers must repay the debt. Inevitably, the result is class struggle; the regimes increase their arms buildup and police forces, and endeavour to infiltrate and corrupt workers' organizations. Subsequently, the workers' leaders are corrupted or co-opted and dictatorships emerge.

He advanced a number of statistics to support his argument, arguing that, in 1982, 40 percent of export earnings in Latin America went to debt repayment, and it is predicted that this figure could rise to 80 percent by 1986.

Jagan claimed that U.S. President Kennedy originally supported him in spite of his Marxist philosophy but eventually unleashed the CIA against him through the trade unions in 1963.

He expressed his support for the Eastern Bloc countries' and the Soviet Union's Marxist integration as an economic model.

Jagan attacked the multinational corporations as destructive to local economies and implied that Third World countries must control their own resources. He said the Puerto Rican model of Arthur Lewis, designed to create an investment climate to attract foreign investment, was exported to Guyana in 1964 and had failed.

He claimed that models exported by the United States are designed to perpetuate world capitalism, as advocated in the Truman Doctrine, and that models of dependent capitalism have only increased the debt load of dependent regions. As a result, the International Monetary Fund invariably demands wage freezes and denationalization, urging a dependent country to put itself on a "capitalist course" with more "free enterprise" as the solution to its problems.

In summation, Jagan said that class struggle, the inevitable result of dependent capitalism, has already surfaced and will continue to develop. The Cuban revolution illustrated the fact that liberation movements may have to turn to friends in the "socialist world" for assistance in facing the anticipated challenge from the capitalist world. The objectives for reform-minded people in the Caribbean must first be to achieve power and to hold power and then to transform the economy. Third World countries cannot afford to stand still, they can only go backward or forward. They must learn to fight and learn with whom to ally themselves to win that fight.

Transcripts of Presentations

Kari Levitt: *Development Models and Theories*

Introduction
I would like to say that I am very pleased to be here, and in the course of my remarks I will elaborate on why I am particularly excited about this conference.

I would like to open my comments by stating the obvious, that there is a lot to be learned from reading and study. However, all the book learning in the world is no substitute for learning from experience. I am bearing in mind recent events in the Caribbean, and most especially those which happened in Grenada in 1983. I would like to appeal for an effort to learn from experience, and to suggest that this effort requires relentless honesty. Learning from experience is difficult, much more difficult than learning from books, because it can be painful and lead us to discard preconceived ideas in which we may have invested a considerable amount of time and energy, and because resilience is required to overcome disappointment and disillusionment and to find the strength to continue in spite of great setbacks. There is no question that the sequence of events in Grenada in 1983 constitute a resounding setback for progressive forces, progressive social change and for sovereign independence in the Caribbean. Any discussion of development models and theories that does not touch base with experience is a waste of time; in fact, it is a form of irresponsibility. Unfortunately I must say that much of what passes as academic scholarship in our universities is precisely that—a waste of time.

I very much welcome the structure of this conference, because it is evident that the intention of its organizers is to confront theories with experience and to exchange ideas within and across cultural boundaries—in this case, the considerable cultural boundaries that divide Atlantic Canada and the Commonwealth Caribbean.

My own learning experience concerning development and underdevelopment, interestingly enough, started simultaneously in Atlantic Canada and in the Caribbean in the year 1960, conveniently the year which your program has chosen to start its review. I first came to Atlantic Canada in the summer of 1960 as a research assistant to Arthur Parks, who was at that time director of research for the Atlantic Provinces Economic Council in Fredericton, New Brunswick. On Christmas 1960, I found myself in the West Indies for the first time, at the Mona campus of the University of the West Indies (U.W.I.) in Jamaica, from whence I was dispatched to Trinidad to dig up information on freight rates in the federal inter-island shipping service. I had the opportunity to observe the process of decolonization from the fourth floor of what was then Federal House but is now Trinidad House in Port of Spain.

I owe my introduction to the Maritimes to Professor Burton Kierstadt, who had recently arrived at the University of Toronto, where I was a graduate student, in his flight from a major row with the administration of McGill University, where he had rebuilt the Department of Economics as chairman. His legacy there remains, as do the rows with the administration.

My introduction to the West Indies I likewise owe to Professor Burton Kierstadt, who had been invited by Sir Arthur Lewis to spend a sabbatical year there and to participate in the production of economic studies that U.W.I. had undertaken for the short-lived federal government of the West Indies. These studies, which continued throughout the 1960s, became a vehicle for younger generations of West Indian economists to lay the foundations for the Caribbean version of what later became known as structural dependency theory. Norman Girvan, in an article now ten years old, explained the relationship of this work to the better-known and more extensive work of Latin American economists, which derived from the path-breaking manifestoes of Paul Prebisch and his co-workers in the 1950s.

I cannot let this occasion pass without a tribute to Burton Kierstadt, a son of the Maritimes, born in Fredericton, where he died some years ago. He was a stimulating and generous teacher, an original mind ready to encourage young scholars and new ideas whether he was in agreement with them or not. He extended moral encouragement and support during his one-year stay at U.W.I. in 1960-61 to young West Indian scholars such as Lloyd Best, Allister MacIntyre and others, whose talents and abilities were perceived as a threat and challenge by the older expatriate elements that still dominated the university.

Atlantic Canada and the Caribbean

I remember a conference held at Dalhousie University in Halifax in 1966 on development problems in the Atlantic Provinces and the West Indies. I recently looked over the paper I had prepared for that occasion on the theme of strategies for economic and social development in underdeveloped regions. Very much of what was in that paper still holds true today.

The two regions clearly share some of the characteristics of peripheral capitalism. This is most clearly demonstrated in the similarity of the subordinate price-taking position of the fishermen of Newfoundland and Nova Scotia with that of the producers of bananas, cocoa, nutmeg or whatever tropical cash crop may be produced in the Caribbean, both groups being under obligation to sell to large companies. There are very many other similarities. The change in the status of Atlantic Canada from its former historic glory in the nineteenth century to its present state as peripheral to Central Canada illustrates the well-known problem of polarization within an economic union. This same problem is well known and much discussed in the Caribbean. There are also important differences in the ways this problem presents itself here and in the Caribbean. The most obvious is that there is a free movement of people from this region to Central Canada and recompensations of various kinds, ranging from subsidized freight rates to equalization payments over which governments may haggle.

The Caribbean experience has some similarities, but it is richer and infinitely more complex and contains more lessons than the experience of the more favoured and fortunate region of Atlantic Canada. This is largely because the Caribbean was where Africa and India intersected with Europe and America, providing the locale for the first and most brutal experiment in the capitalist exploitation of unfree labour. This legacy remains a conditioning factor.

The Caribbean has since experienced the acquisition of political independence by virtually all of its islands and territories, with but one exception. Unfortunately it happens to be located in a region considered by one of the two superpowers as its privileged backyard. The most recent victims of this backyard problem were the people of Grenada, whose bold experiment in new forms of social organization and motivation was brutally cut in 1983 in a series of events intimately connected with the crosscurrents of the superpowers.

Models of Development
I have been asked to talk about models and theories of development. In the 1980s, the emphasis surely must be on rethinking, given the ferocious impact of the current world crisis on the living standards of peoples throughout the Third World. We have no time to listen to repetitions of the old and tired phrases that we have heard year in and year out. We have to look back, to learn and think.

Think for a moment about the phenomenon the newspapers blandly call "the debt problem" and the programs imposed on the people of these so-called better countries such as Mexico, Brazil, the Philippines, Jamaica or any one of the other dozens of countries where, under the innocent and bland-sounding "stabilization programs," there has been a transfer of real resources from the poor to the rich. Within these countries, the burden has fallen brutally and heavily on those least able to bear it.

The Economic Commission for Latin America stated that in the last two years there has been a net transfer of $50 billion from Latin America to the commercial banks alone. This figure represents the difference between interest on the principal paid and any new loans extended over the past two years.

The living standards of people have been savagely slashed. I could not begin to put into words the kind of conditions which obtain, to the point of malnutrition and starvation, in countries where such things never happened before, and this includes Mexico. It is an intolerable and enormous injustice, and this point merits some thinking about. The people who are bearing the burden of the repayment of these loans are not the same people who principally benefitted from the obtaining of the loans. (I am not now speaking of the banks and finance companies who were immensely greedy in pushing these loans upon their borrowers and pushing us deeper into debt. I am speaking of the borrowers.) Examine what some of the financed projects were, who benefitted from them and who was able to stash away large amounts of money into foreign bank accounts. When you look at who is paying for these loans, it is the masses of the people. In Mexico, in one year alone—and Mexico is a very large country—there was a reduction in average real wages and salaries of 25 percent. This is an average figure— you can imagine what this means in real malnutrition, real poverty, real absence of medical services and so on.

This crisis often has been compared with that of the 1930s. The situation in the so-called developed, industrialized countries is not good. We know that. There is an economic crisis of a kind. Growth has slowed. There is unemployment, inflation and other things, but in no way are conditions in the developed countries comparable to what happened in the 1930s in North America or Europe. However, the reports that reach us from Latin America and increasingly from the Caribbean, particularly Jamaica and the Dominican Republic, would indicate that the situation there has never been so bad. The only comparison is the thirties, and in some ways things are worse than they were in the 1930s because people are less self-reliant and more dependent on all kinds of structures of so-called development than they were then, and are less able to feed themselves. This, of course, is a worldwide phenomenon. Everybody is less self-reliant, everybody is more interdependent for food and all sorts of necessities of life.

Given the crisis that has overcome this world, we need to free ourselves from the constraints we might tend to impose on our own thinking, particularly those constraints that arise from the major contending ideologies. We must understand the world as it really is and regard with great suspicion all theories of what I would call economic determinism, whether advanced from the political Right in terms of the innate technological or cultural superiority of industrialized countries, or from the political Left in the form of supposed scientific laws of historical materialism in which events appear to be more determinant than they really are. I am making a plea for opening our minds, looking at history and understanding that the outcome of struggle is much less determinant than many people think. It is very much more, therefore, in the hands of people to influence developments.

We have to look realistically at the failure of various kinds of models, various kinds of social experiments, both those favoured by the political Left and those favoured by the political Right. Any discussion of development models cannot proceed in a simplistic and foolish way as if development models were something like motor-car models which we can pick and choose—I like this and I don't like that. As people become disenchanted with this year's favourite model, they find new favourites and new models, followed, of course, by new disillusionments and new enchantments.

Decolonization has proceeded very quickly in the past 30 years. There has been a parade of models. Some of you may be able to remember the attractions. In its golden years, a model would attract a stream of pilgrims and camp followers to offer assistance to the latest social experiment and then to cry over the failure of whatever kinds of hopes people had pinned on the efforts of poor people to assist themselves. We need only to recall Nigeria after independence, Cuba in the early years of the revolution, revolutionary Grenada, and Nicaragua. For those who incline to the political Right, there has been the Puerto Rico model, and the miracle of Brazil before it collapsed, and currently the gang of four is in high fashion—Taiwan, South Korea, Hong Kong and Singapore. We have been treated to all sorts of schemes to make one Caribbean country or another into a Singapore or Hong Kong (I do not know which of these was Mr. Seaga's dream). China, after three decades as a favourite model for people interested in social change, is now finding favour in business circles because it has made a very big turn in policy. History tells us that this is not likely to be the last major shift in China.

Like other people, I am often asked, "What development model do *you* favour?" And I refuse to answer this question. I find it impossible to answer, because the question is meaningless when it is outside a context of time and place and, moreover, it is profoundly disrespectful of the struggles of peoples to escape poverty and underdevelopment. Each time a model country or a leader of such a country falls from the pedestal of its well-meaning admirers, the people of the country concerned vanish from the newspapers and journals and the attention of the spectators shifts to some other spot or cause to wave flags at. Such an approach exposes our appalling lack of a sense of history, which would moderate our preconceptions of what is possible at any given time in any given place.

Abstracting from cultural factors leads people to believe that models are necessarily transferable from one part of the world to another. This underestimation of cultures reflects a kind of ethnocentric economic determinism which downgrades cultural factors as mobilizing forces. In reality, cultural forces are perhaps the greatest source of social cohesion and an essential mechanism for individual and social survival.

My argument then is that there is indeed a crisis in the nations that have been scarred by colonialism and enmeshed in the worldwide economic network of neo-colonialism, not to mention military invasion. Such is currently the case in Central America and southern Africa. The solution to this crisis cannot be burdened by the constraints of ideologies born in other places and other circumstances, especially when these ideologies are manipulated by superpowers for their own political ends.

Without question there is such a thing as a world capitalist system. It is based on the sanctity of property—private property, but perhaps later, state property—the primacy of capital over labour and of money over people. As an old Hungarian proverb has it: "Money talks, dogs bark." We need to understand how the system functions, and we need to understand that it is buttressed by the rules of the game embodied in the international institutions that powerful interests have erected for the protection of the international system of trade, investment and payments. We need to understand the rules of the game and the primacy of force, the primacy of international economic relations over national self-determined sovereignty and indigenously or nationally determined political and social institutions. The leash with which peripheral countries, most of which are small, are kept under control always has to do with the foreign exchange situation, the balance of payment problem. That is the ultimate way these countries are brought into line, with policies imposed by the bankers, the International Monetary Fund and related institutions.

Liberation must be a triumph of politics over economics. Prices, exchange rates, interest rates and so forth, the stuff of economics, are reflections of the underlying power relations among countries. The prices that rule international markets are not facts of nature. If we really understand economics, we will understand that it reflects *power* relations. It goes all the way back to the time when the British grabbed up most of the territory in the world—the empty lands of North America, Australia, New Zealand, Argentina, South Africa, Kenya. The French helped themselves to some of it too, and settled Europeans there. That was in the era when division of the world's land was determined by military power. Sir Arthur Lewis, the greatest economist the Caribbean has produced, has explained in a very few words, particularly in the Schumpeter lectures delivered in 1977, and more clearly than anyone else has explained in long books, the inequity of the international system and the basic reason for it, largely the one I just mentioned.

Cheddi Jagan: *Development Models and Theories*

I will begin by recalling a trip to Ottawa when I was premier. As I entered the room, the prime minister pointed to me with his finger and said, "Young man, we are not going to allow communists anywhere in the Commonwealth." And that is what they would not allow in 1953 when it was said that the People's Progressive Party (PPP) wanted to set up a communist state within the British Empire. In 1965, when the Americans landed 45,000 troops in the Dominican Republic, Lyndon Johnson said the same thing, the United States would not allow any communists to come to power in any part of the hemisphere after the Cuban revolution. So, in discussing models and theories, we have put things into perspective.

Sometimes we talk about the Caribbean as exceptional. The Caribbean has been brought together by peoples who were uprooted from elsewhere and came there with a particular culture and so on. I have just heard something about this part of Canada, which I am not too familiar with. The Caribbean needs to compare its particular regional or interstate experiences with historical experiences elsewhere, for instance, in Canada. Reference was made to Canada being a middle power. Well, Russia under the czars was perhaps a middle power too. In fact, that is why the Russian revolution took place, because the people were starving under czarist feudalism and a very backward type of capitalism. Within backward capitalism there were areas that were very backward. That is what we are talking about here too. The Russians went ahead in backward areas, having established workers' power, soviet power, to eliminate that backwardness by bypassing capitalism, taking what Lenin called the noncapitalist road to socialism. So, it is not hopeless. We are backward here in Atlantic Canada. The thing to do is to fight against the system. State monopoly capitalism, which you have here, is linked up with the United States. Being in a peripheral position creates problems for underdeveloped regions such as Atlantic Canada.

Now back to the Caribbean. We wanted to bring about change. I grew up on a plantation. I knew exactly what poverty, etc., meant. So when we wanted change, it was said that we wanted to set up a communist state.

We have to relate that now to the Second World War and the immediate postwar era. The Soviet Union helped to win the war and defeat world fascism. In the process it helped to liberate Eastern Europe, which was like eastern Canada in relation to the rest of Canada. It was underdeveloped and backward relative to Western Europe. Backward peripheral areas always exist within the capitalist structure. So that part was liberated. Winston Churchill was then prime minister. Socialism was given a mandate in the 1945 elections, and Churchill was unable to come back to power. Before leaving, he got together with Truman and declared communism was going too far. Eastern Europe was liberated. They were forced to give India freedom when the Atlantic Charter was proclaimed in 1944 and Roosevelt wanted to concede independence to India. Churchill at the time said he was not appointed the king's first minister to preside over the liquidation of the British Empire. However, India was given its freedom, but not before it was partitioned. So Churchill and Truman got together and decided to stop the world from advancing. No more revolutions.

That is what we must understand when we begin talking about models. Before the Truman Doctrine was proclaimed, Truman stated that governments which conducted planned economies and controlled foreign trades were dangerous to freedom, speaking, of course, of the Soviet Union. He said freedom of speech and worship were dependent on the free-enterprise system, and the controlled economies were not the American way and not the way to peace. He urged the whole world to adopt the American system and said the American system could survive in America only if it became a world system. Calling for action, he implored, unless we act decisively, government-controlled economies and government-controlled foreign trade will be the pattern for the next century, and if this trend is not reversed the government of the United States will be under pressure, sooner or later, to use the same devices to fight for markets and raw materials. So, at the end of the war, the United States assumed the mantle of world imperialism. Britain and all the other imperialist countries were devastated. The United States was very wealthy and so it assumed the responsibility of derailing revolution.

The first act of the Truman Doctrine was to shore up Turkey and Greece to bring back the monarch and the corrupt leaders to stop revolution there the same way Ronald Reagan is trying to stop revolution in Nicaragua, El Salvador and Guatemala. History is repeating itself. This is how the PPP government fell in 1953 and this is why the liberal Kennedy administration unleashed the U.S. Central Intelligence Agency (CIA) against us in the 1960s with the slogan, No More Cubas in the Western Hemisphere. This was the same slogan that led to the overthrow of the Allende government, the Goulart government in Brazil, the Manley government and more recently the Grenada revolution. All this started with the Truman Doctrine, which aimed to export the system of world monopoly capitalism all over the world and to make the whole world become dependencies in a new form: neo-colonialism.

And the models were waiting. First, the Puerto Rican one. What is the theory behind it? You haven't got money, but you need money for development. Therefore you must create an investment climate to attract this money and give all kinds of incentives: tax holidays, duty-free concessions, etc. So we enter a rat race to invite this or that foreign capitalist to come to develop our countries. We start with five-year tax holidays, then some give seven, then some give ten, others give fifteen, and some say, come along, you don't have to pay any taxes with us. Indeed, why not, because they put in one dollar and take out four. That is the history of Latin America. Then the government, because of the suffering of the people, borrows more money and also is told to build roads, sea defences and infrastructure, which all become an added help to the imperialists. So today we have this big debt problem.

In Guyana, the CIA removed us and installed Forbes Burnham. Before being installed he had been the first minister of education in my first government. After he lost two elections, the CIA installed him in power and poured money into the country—actually, into the hands of corrupt politicians who are only interested in themselves. But that is part of the imperialist job, in order to plunder resources, people and everything else. As I said, they sow one dollar and reap four in all Third World countries today through interest, profits, unequal international trading, sale of royalties, etc.—$100 billion to $120 billion have come out of Guyana. So these countries borrow and keep borrowing. Then they are told to put it into infrastructure. You borrow over 12-25 years but the recovery of that capital from infrastructure takes 50-100 years. So you keep attacking the workers and the working people to find the money to pay that debt. Then the class struggle sharpens. These regimes then build bigger and bigger armies to hold onto the people. Then they resort to fraud in general elections and in trade-union elections, to control the workers so they do not strike. So you have a process where dictatorships set in. Finally the International Monetary Fund (IMF) comes in with what is called a rescue operation to give you some money. They give it to you with one hand and take it out with the other.

From 1975 in Guyana more money was going out than was coming in as loans. That is the problem. Juscelino Kubitschek, president of Brazil, said that Latin America was like a sick man receiving blood transfusions and donating blood at the same time. The debt payments of Guyana are now $521 million. In 1964 it was $10 million, but that is not the big fact. The big fact is that the $521 million of debt represents 92 percent of all revenues— 92 percent of revenues collected from the people through taxation goes to pay debts. This is an impossible situation. And every year it is going up. According to the Economic Commission for Latin America (ECLA) the foreign debt payment for the whole of Latin America two years ago was 40 percent of all foreign earnings. A University of California at Berkeley study showed that if the same process were to continue to 1986, debt payments would be around 80 percent of foreign earnings.

So what is to be done? For models, we had not only the Puerto Rican model but the Alliance for Progress, which lost its way because it was based on wishful thinking, calling upon Latin American oligarchies to reform themselves. Kennedy was an enlightened exponent of his class. He wanted capitalism to survive as a system. But the oil barons, steel barons, and so on in Latin America wanted to make quick kills. So Kennedy was called a socialist and a communist although he was no such thing, and eventually they shot him too. As I said, he unleashed the CIA against us. When he saw Khrushchev in 1961, Kennedy said, look at Jagan, he won his position in an election and he is a Marxist, but we respect that. Two years later, the CIA was unleashed against us through the trade-union movement, which they smashed illegally and put under the control of the American Institute of Free Labor Development (AIFLD), which organized an 80-day strike financed by the CIA against the government in 1963. So this is what we are up against. If you attempt to change the structure, whether in Guyana in my time or in Nicaragua or Chile, you are in trouble.

After the Alliance for Progress failed, there was the ECLA model of import substitution, which also did not produce any results. It was still based on foreign capital. You had regional integration, and this has to be seen in the context of the progress made in the socialist world, which has been experiencing a rate of growth about twice as large as in the capitalist world. Because the East had the Council for Mutual Economic Assistance (COMECON), the West had to develop a similar organization for economic co-operation. In order to specialize, to become more efficient in competition with the East and to take advantage of the technological and scientific revolution, common markets were established in Europe, the Caribbean, Central America and so on. This was in the interest of the transnational corporations as well because they were not interested in going into every country to set up a factory, especially when factories were getting bigger and bigger. If you have a free-trade area or a common market to go to, one place, set it up there and control the whole area.

The argument for regional interaction was that we would benefit, we would have the advantage of the economics of scale. But after the transnational corporations have destroyed the local bourgeoisie through unfair methods, they become monopolies and charge what the market will bear. That also helps to exploit and plunder us. So much for the ECLA model.

In 1973, after the oil crisis, and with the Third World countries beginning to talk about nationalization and controlling their own resources, the West turned to a new model: joint ventures. Since private people do not have enough money, even states and governments can come into partnerships. So we had under this model what Eduardo Frei called the Chileanization of copper. Not denationalization but 49-51 percent ownership, along the lines of the Puerto Rican model, which in 1964 Arthur Lewis had brought into the whole Caribbean until it crumbled. By 1970-71 the Caribbean was already in a crisis situation (what had saved us from 1904-71 had been the high prices in the sugar markets in the world). Then they began talking about co-operative socialism. Like Chileanization of copper in Chile, the slogan in Guyana was "majority participation in bauxite," the partnership model.

All these models that were exported not just to the Caribbean but to the whole world were intended to perpetuate capitalism, as Truman argued back in 1947, to make the world system the same as the capitalist system in the United States of America—but dependent capitalism. That is why today, with the world crisis of capitalism, we are feeling it more, because the colonial economic structure has not changed very much. In fact it has gotten worse. In Guyana we had three products in the colonial period: sugar, rice and bauxite. They are still there and after 20 years we are producing less of those three products than we did in 1964. Despite all the money that has come into the country, we are up to our necks in debt. So the model has not succeeded.

How to fight back, how to change? If you try to change, the Americans will send in the marines or the CIA or what is called the destabilizing economic blockade. Then the IMF comes in and says, denationalize, solve the budget crisis at the expense of the people, freeze wages, cut social services (social services declined from 45 percent in 1964 to 22 percent in 1983) and put your country on a capitalist course. Right now the pressure in Guyana is to denationalize, to go from a bureaucratic, dependent form of capitalism to a free-enterprise type. This has failed already in Latin America. It lead to revolution in Cuba, it led to revolution in Nicaragua and so on. And that is where Reagan is trying to push Guyana at the moment. We say, no, don't denationalize, democratize! Power is held through fraud, through the military, without democracy, with discrimination, corruption, extravagance. So we have a problem. As the people struggle, the USA wants to back these regimes maintaining corrupt power and to build up the army and police for use against the workers. I heard a broadcast with Reagan and his democratic competitor Mondale on the question of the Philippines. Reagan virtually said, we have to back people like Marcos, in other words, back all the dictators like Pinochet or whomever, because we are afraid of communism.

I came to this question: We have to fight the class struggle and win national liberation, but how to win?

I do not agree with some of my colleagues in the Caribbean and Atlantic Canada. If we want to win, we not only have to understand international politics but we have to be realists too. Fidel Castro could not have survived without having been a realist. He won alone. To transform the economy, to go from a national liberation revolution to a socialist revolution, he had to come in conflict with the United States and the CIA with the Bay of Pigs invasion, and he had to turn to the Soviet Union for help—economic help, military help, political help.

The same process that started in Guyana in 1953 ended in the 1960s with Vietnam. How did the Vietnamese win? First, the Communists created a broad unity in the country, uniting other parties, trade unions, youths, farmers, women, everybody. Second, they had close co-operation with the socialist world. Sometimes I hear distinctions about bureaucratic this and that and so on. But that is socialism. Had these distinctions not been forgotten, the Vietnamese would not have won. Third, the Vietnamese made peace and friendship with the working class and the democratic forces for peace in the capitalist world, including Americans who fought against their own government. We have to keep this in mind: (1) get power, (2) hold power and (3) transform. If we forget this we are not going to succeed.

We, especially the Caribbean, are in what is referred to as the USA's backyard. It is not going to be easy. Some people in this situation develop an opportunistic, pragmatic position: if you can't beat them, join them. I say, join them for what? We have no choice. The Third World countries cannot stand still. You either go backward or go forward. To join them means you only become like the puppets in these client states who eventually become dictators and kill people, torturing them to maintain their power. We have to fight but we have to learn how to fight and with whom to ally in order to win.

Commentary by Miguel Murmis

by Peter MacLellan

The discussant, **Miguel Murmis** (Sociology, University of Toronto), began by looking at the perspective from which each speaker addressed the issue of development models. **Levitt**, he noted, approached it as an academic committed to social change but preferring to participate in the process solely as an academic, helping people to define problems and solutions. **Sacouman** went a step further in seeking a more active bridge between academia and the process of change by linking up with specific social and political struggles. And **Jagan** spoke from an even more activist stance, as a decision-maker, as someone committed to participation in the struggle for change within a leadership role.

Murmis said some of the disagreements among the three speakers in their approach to development (the need for theoretical models, etc.) have to do with their different roles in the process of social change. Thus Levitt approached each situation with intellectual commitment but limited herself to understanding the situation and to helping people project a meaningful future. She searched for patterns in constraints and goals, liberation needs, but agonized over the limitations of all experiments, without a clear orientation towards any theoretical model for change, and counselled the avoidance of pre-established models. Sacouman insisted on the need to engage in action, action guided by models and not by chance, related to classes and groups (e.g., small producers) that are relatively marginal at the moment but with the best potential for the construction of a new future. Murmis noted that it was not by chance that Jagan introduced his remarks about the transition and the road to decisions with a call for realism. If you want to have real change, you have to know what the international setting is, and there is little room for manoeuvre here with respect to alliances and so on.

In this positioning of the three speakers, Murmis aligned himself more or less with Levitt with respect to the relevance of available models and to the powerful constraints on people's efforts to change their situation. In pursuing these questions, Murmis responded to points made by the three speakers along three lines: (1) how to conceptualize problems of development associated with the location of countries in the international division of labour and with changes in the form of dependency, (2) the internal structure of dependency within underdeveloped countries and regions and (3) the viable options for change within social structures that are modeled on experiences elsewhere.

He continued (transcript):

It is not by chance that Levitt started with the question of debt and that Jagan emphasized it so much. Paradoxically, the increase in debt tends to make the reality of dependency, in the way we used to think about it, less clear. Why? Because not only in Argentina but also in other Latin American countries, increased debt is coupled with less direct investment. Jagan noted that for Guyana—and this is also true for Argentina—the decamping of foreign investment gave the impression that dependency was receding. It is interesting to see how Sacouman's discussion of Atlantic Canada, although concentrating on a completely different mechanism of dependency, also emphasized forms of dependency in which direct investment is not the central mechanism.

This brings us back to an old story: If one wants to recognize dependency, one has to look for it. We have to understand that it is not only a change in stages of capitalist development—from sheer plunder to mercantile and financial dependence, to direct investment, etc.—but that there are new stages or at least new forms that in a sense go back to some of the old forms and at the same time give the old forms new meaning. One of the central facts about this debt is that it is difficult to identify the internal forces that are responsible for the debt. It is very difficult to find the foreign investor in the country. It is not by chance that one of the most radical revolutions of recent times, the Nicaraguan revolution, took place in a country where direct investment was not that significant. Even compared with other Central American countries, direct involvement of foreign capital in Nicaragua was minimal. We have another example, Cuba, where direct investments were central.

So, how do we predict revolution, or socialism, in countries where direct investment is essential? How do we predict revolutions in countries where direct investment is not powerful? We have to think about how the external power acts internally and find the specific forms in each case. This does not mean there is no general model. A model identifies theories of alternative forms of action, but we have to find the most decisive form of penetration at a specific time and understand how this form of penetration is connected to the internal structure of a country.

An important factor must be borne in mind. If we have forms of penetration where direct investment is not that clear or immediate, then we have two consequences. One consequence was clear in Sacouman's presentation: how do we analyse the internal structure of a country, the basic social forces, there? If the external presence is not expressed directly through capital, is that the end of proletarian exploitation? Does it mean that the only alternative is the unity of the forces in the dependent country or region? This is the first consequence.

The other consequence is that the internal structure becomes much more complex. It is not just that you have a few foreign capitalists controlling investments, exploited peasants and workers, and a few merchants. No. Insofar as foreign capital is not there, what we have is the development of all sorts of class fractions and, as Sacouman explained in the case of Atlantic Canada, a situation in which exploited people are not fully proletarianized. In many countries we have the old problem of the peasantry and the working class. What we find is a nucleus of fully proletarianized workers and different sorts of exploited people who are not fully proletarianized. What new class alliances can be established when class structures have become so complex? What sectors of the internal bourgeoisie really benefitted from the expansion of the debt and dependency? This again changes from country to country. What we find is that models are useful for posing relevant questions but not for providing the answers.

Who should ally with whom? First we have to analyse the structure of exploitation and find out what happens to the surplus. How is it channelled outside? What is the role of the bourgeoisie, in its various class fractions, in the different productive sectors? What we find is that it is necessary to build new strategies for development, strategies with not only a redefinition of classes but also a redefinition of what is good and bad in productive activity.

Here the question of the relationship between agriculture and industry can be raised—for instance, the old question that Jagan raised about the extent to which dependent countries should move away from the pattern of dependence on natural resources, and Sacouman's reference to the important role of natural resources development in Atlantic Canada. It is important to find different answers to the old questions, especially within the Economic Commission for Latin America's tradition where it was assumed that agriculture was basically backward because it was controlled by big landowners, and what can the peasants do? We can help them survive, let them subsist, but development has to move in other directions.

One of the surprising facts about discussions among the Left in Latin America, especially on the structure of production, is how little attention is paid to Cuba and Nicaragua. In Cuba, the initial experiment in industrialization was later redefined. In Nicaragua, there was a clear decision about which sectors had to expand. We cannot discuss the question here, but the alternatives are open on the question of export agriculture versus production for the internal market. There is discussion about more concentrated agriculture, be it through corporations or state-help versus help to the peasants, and about the question of subsistence versus production for the market. There are very real alternatives that people have to face, and this is something common to Atlantic Canada and most of the underdeveloped countries. This is not just an economic question. It is also a social question that has to do with the way social alliances are formed. How do we take into account the fact that the fisheries and agriculture are so essential in Atlantic Canada? What kind of alliances can we build there? What future can be predicted on the basis of these alliances?

These questions relate to the first problem—the changing forms of dependency—posed by Moore and the fact that, within some of the new forms of dependency, direct investment is not as visible.

The second topic is: Is it possible to think of some exploited groups as central? Or do we have to accept models of a clash between proletarians and petty producers? Is it possible to establish larger alliances?

The third topic is central in Jagan's presentation. Although we have to remember that countries act in an international setting, the discussion is about the internal social forces that represent a progressive alliance and, to a large extent, the connection with the external world is conditioned by that. In countries where the bourgeoisie is formed in the process of dependent associated capitalism, many sectors are very well organized, and an established working class wants to have a say in defining the new model. They have their own preferences, not only among possible international alliances but among possible consequences of international alignments for the internal structure. All over Latin America, the concern with establishing forms of participatory democracy, by which different fractions of the society find ways of expressing their views and entering into conflict within the process of change, is becoming more central.

In Argentina, through political struggle, class struggle and armed struggle, people are trying to find a way for the process of change to bring together different sectors of the population, and this includes a commitment to pluralism after the change. This is a central topic of discussion in Chile today, for instance. They are trying to see how pluralism can be established. That is why the Nicaraguans explain that pluralism is so relevant all over Latin America, and that is why we are so concerned with the way it moves in the future. In many cases, this clashes with an alignment with the Soviet Union, for instance. The internal project could clash with models that come from the state socialist countries. This is the first point we should bear in mind. It is clear that we won't get any support from the imperialist centre. It is also clear that relations with state socialist countries represent problems, not only in international alignments but also in the consequences they bring to the internal model. That is one point.

The second point is that no struggle can really be won on the basis of external support. This was the experience of Allende's Chile. It's not possible to count on external support. Perhaps some areas of the world can, and if they want to, nice for them, but not everybody can count on that, and this is one reason why the minister of agriculture in the Sandinista government expresses a desire to maintain relations with countries outside the socialist world. They do not want Nicaragua to get its oil from the Soviet Union because they don't want to build a pipeline to the Soviet Union and, besides, even if they wanted to, they could not. So that immediately brings a redefinition of the way a country establishes its presence at the international level. Our experience in Argentina is not encouraging in the kind of international support that can be obtained. Because of certain reasons, during the Argentine dictatorship, the Soviet Union supported the dictatorship and opposed the discussion of human rights questions in Argentina and international forums. I don't think that this is so terrible, because I think that Argentine's struggle is one thing and the deployment of international power is something else. In some cases both things overlap, and in some cases they don't.

So, the central task is one that perhaps Sacouman tried to underline for us: to provide analysis that makes it possible for academics to participate in the formation of progressive alliances that will start moving forward within the conditions of a country. Moving forward in Atlantic Canada means generating the basis of social movements on the basis of historical experience. Perhaps moving forward in Guyana means trying to establish critical opposition to an existing government. Moving forward in other countries means engaging in armed revolutions. Different tasks require different types of international connections.

Summation by Panelists

by Peter MacLellan

Levitt disagreed with Sacouman's "zoo theory,"' stating that capitalism did not need poor people or cheap labour. She said that it is difficult to categorize people and that one should be careful in the use of Marxist terminology. Levitt did not accept what she called Jagan's "Godfather theory," i.e., if you can't live with Uncle Sam, then call for help from the USSR. She said Jagan did not acknowledge the decline of superpower influence she claims is currently happening. In summation, she reiterated that one must recognize reality and not be trapped in a web of ideology and rhetoric.

Sacouman said that "capitalist zoos" are not a statement of dogma but a reflection of reality.

Jagan summed up his arguments with three main points: (1) monopoly capitalism constantly moves to areas of cheaper labour, (2) unemployment is growing and (3) the Soviet Union is a true supporter of liberation movements. He concluded that revolutionary groups must build alliances to maximize their strength and influence.

Question Period: It was often difficult to ascertain the questioner and the nature of the question. However, certain interests did emerge, such as (1) whether models failed because they were misapplied, inappropriate or structurally unsound; (2) an attempt to differentiate between functionalist arguments concerning capitalism and the general tendencies of the capitalist system, e.g. labour pools, are they a function or a result of capitalist exploitation; and (3) the notion that the emergence of socialism is a prerequisite for effective feminism.

In answer to one question concerning models, **Levitt** stated that she would approve of any model that featured a mixed economy, a pluralistic society and a nonaligned foreign policy. She rejected the notion of a state party and pointed to Hungary and Austria as illustrations of how nations can escape stereotypes to achieve working societal models.

REGIONAL DEVELOPMENT: ISSUES AND RESOURCES

Summary of Presentations

by Chairperson Rudolphe Lamarche

This workshop generated considerable interest. It was unfortunate that Norman Girvan of the United Nations Centre for Development Projects was unable to attend, as his participation would have provided considerable insight into UN efforts to reduce world economic disparities. However, the panel did a thorough job of outlining the issues of and resources for regional development in the Caribbean and Atlantic Canada.

Herb Addo (Institute of International Relations, University of the West Indies, Trinidad) made a presentation (abstract follows) that linked the morning and afternoon sessions. He described how the use of European models and concepts in a Caribbean environment make it difficult to define regional issues in a manner acceptable to the region's population, and how the resources of the Caribbean were at a disadvantage within such a European concept. However, he was left with little time to describe a better modeling procedure for the Caribbean.

Ramesh Ramsaran (International Economic Relations, Institute of International Relations, Trinidad) stressed that the current international economic organization makes it extremely difficult for small Caribbean entrepreneurs to make headway against the multinationals, and also makes it extremely difficult for the region to promote its own development.

Dan MacInnes (Sociology, St. Francis Xavier University, Nova Scotia) described the numerous attempts made by the Canadian government to reduce regional disparities in the Atlantic Provinces, and how difficult it has been, and still is, to overcome the geographical barriers to growth.

Tom Kent (ex–first deputy minister of the federal Department for Regional Economic Expansion, Canada) described the practical issues of launching and implementing development programs in a federal state. He also described the enormous impact that changes in the overall national economic situation will have on regional disparities in Canada.

Ken Higgins (currently a Fellow of the Canadian Institute for Research and Regional Development) made an important contribution by depicting the differences between regional research in Canada and that in the international community. In Canada, regional development nearly always is seen as in opposition to national development. In other countries, regional development is planned into the overall national development scheme.

Abstract of Paper Presented

Herb Addo: *Crisis in the Development Praxis: A Global Perspective*

(An edited version of this paper can be found in a companion volume to this publication, *Rethinking Caribbean Development* [Halifax: International Education Centre, Saint Mary's University, 1987])

After 40 years of pursuing "development," there is a crisis in the praxis of development, and a debate has opened between those who say that the Third World cannot develop and those who say it is developing and will continue to do so.

On one side, New Left Marxists think that development is happening and that any development crisis simply reflects a general crisis in the world economy. On the other side, neo-Marxists of the world-system school insist that capitalist development as such is not possible in Third World societies precisely because of the capitalist nature of the modern world-system, and that the crisis in the praxis of development is a permanent part of world history. I fully share this latter view.

If there is a crisis in the development project, the source of this crisis is largely the basic development philosophy and its epistemological foundations (the validating anchor of knowledge and its application) from which theories and policies of development derive their legitimacy.

The problem is this: the philosophy, methodology and epistemology of development presently derives from a specific, yet universally prescribed and applied, cultural approach to development. To resolve the crisis in the praxis of development, movement from this specific cultural conception of development to an historical understanding of cultural ideas of development is called for.

The first task is to ascertain the extent to which the economic performance of the Third World deviates from what was anticipated, and whether the development project is performing well, underperforming, non-performing, or producing the opposite of what was intended.

Evaluating the Performance of the Development Project
Those who believe that capitalist development is not only possible but in fact going on in the Third World argue that, at least in some countries, capitalist development is proceeding at a realistic pace, with "warts and

all." If development performance lags behind expectations, it is a fault of the expectations. The spokesman for this point of view is Bill Warren, who makes the stark case that, at this phase of world history, imperialism is capitalistically developing Third World societies. Imperialism does this by spearheading the destruction of resistance to capitalist modernization, by diffusing resistance to capitalist modernization, by diffusing whatever is needed to develop capitalism to these societies, by developing the productive forces of Third World countries, and by increasing proletarianization. In the course of this process, standards of living (the humane conditions of life) are improving. He is unimpressed by the argument that the historical mission of imperialism has not been to develop Third World societies but to exploit them. He finds it curious that many scholars do not recognize the progressive side and historical familiarity of Third World experience.

As Samir Amin has noted, however, capital found on the periphery is not derived from autocentred capital accumulation. Comprador capital is always ready to flee to the First World at the slightest sign of instabilities in the world system. Can imperialism create anything other than "nervous" capital, even in the most dynamic Third World countries? As Andre Gunder Frank's "development of underdevelopment" thesis, Amin's "peripheral capitalism" thesis, and Immanuel Wallerstein's "limited possibilities of transformation" thesis have argued, external forces have primacy over internal forces in the uneven expansion of capitalism on the periphery.

In contrast to Warren's argument that industrial capitalism has emerged in the "newly industrialized countries" (NICs) and will soon emerge elsewhere, I assert that there has been "growth without development" and increasing marginalization, polarization and immiseration on a world scale. The extent of industrial progress Warren claims to see in the NICs has been successfully disputed elsewhere by James Petras, and even where developmental gains have been achieved, progress is threatened by a heavy debt burden. The countries often cited as those industrializing and hence developing are those most heavily in debt. We have an absurd situation in which the more a country is supposed to be industrializing, the more it has borrowed and the more it needs to produce to service its external debt. How can even the handful of NICs accumulate enough capital to sustain developmental gains, much less the "unfortunate" many? The austerity programs imposed on Third World countries by the International Monetary Fund and other financial institutions as a means of meeting foreign debt obligations does not consolidate but rather undermines and even rolls back any progress made. No single Third World country or group of them has a capitalist development formula that can be recommended as a successful model for other Third World countries to emulate.

Furthermore, the comparison of the miserable conditions in the Third World with conditions in earlier periods of capitalist development in Europe must cease. This comparison is merely a case of vulgar determinism and amounts to a nonprogressive refusal to apply the benefits of historical experience to living human beings. What is going on in the Third World does not approximate or even resemble the classical capitalist development of the developed world but is at best a bastardized form of earlier capitalist development: *peripheral capitalism*, complete with an historically endowed lack of autocentred dynamism. The performance of Third World "development" has been dubious at best.

The failure of expectations is rooted in the untenability of a particular cultural approach to development, and this culture's dominance in applying its idea. This approach has been based on Eurocentric values, images, epistemology and models (see Figure 1).

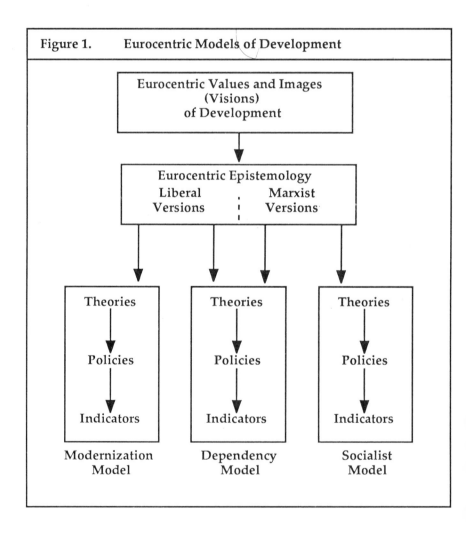

Figure 1.   Eurocentric Models of Development

Rethinking Development

Every society has certain values and images which represent what that society considers to be the meaning of "development." Development policies are authentic or valid only when the relationship between the image of development and the bases of a society's "cultures" is organic. When development policies fail persistently over long periods of time and the failure cannot be accounted for fully by distortions in or misdeductions from theories, the explanation for the failure must be traced back beyond the level of theory to the level of epistemology and methodology, to problems with the particular images of development.

The blame for developmental failure falls largely if not exclusively on the nature of conventional theories of development. In effect, we have only three basic competing models of development: (1) modernization, (2) dependency and (3) socialist. These three models are more similar than they are different. They share common Eurocentric development values, images and epistemological foundations. Their basic source is European experiences in the modern world. These models assume that to develop, Third World societies must adopt European values and repeat European stages of modern history. This is at once arrogant, overbearing, bigoted, repugnant, untrue, racist and contemptible.

Even one holding the Eurocentric socialist vision of desirable society would argue that all societies must industrialize, as they did in Europe, to enhance human dignity and welfare. This way to the development of Third World societies has failed, and failed miserably. This must be admitted if we are to proceed further with our rethinking of development. Third World societies cannot develop along conventional lines because, by adopting Eurocentic models, they deprive themselves of the internal autonomy necessary for controlling, generating and accumulating capital. Also, in general, the desirability of trying to Europeanize is highly problematic. It is imperative that we look elsewhere when rethinking development in the Third World.

We need to expand beyond the strict confines of conventional Eurocentric terms of reference. We need to reopen the development debate in a much broader form and at a much higher level. This demands the unearthing of other, suppressed images of development to enrich present conventional values, images, and theories. We need to anchor the humanizing process of development in the authentic and vital cultural contexts of Third World societies themselves.

Keynote Addresses

Robert Moore: *Canada and the Caribbean in a World of Crises*

(Robert Moore is a past high commissioner of Guyana to Canada)

The crises of the 1980s are older than the 1980s, but at the moment they are being revealed in extremely sharp focus, and the focus is getting sharper as this decade proceeds. I will briefly review three crises we have been talking about since last night, to create a framework for the observations I want to make.

The first crisis is the debt crisis. It was observed this morning that something like $625 billion is owed by a number of Third World countries to banks in the First World.

The debt crisis is symptomatic of a second, deeper crisis, and that is the crisis of the old international economic order. People in the Third World, in particular the poor, are feeling the effects of the debt crisis, and debt has become yet another way for the Third World to finance the First. The debtor becomes the beneficiary of the creditors. As one banker recently put it, "Where there is debt, there is hope." If the debt crisis is simply a symptom of the decay of the old international economic order, that order is showing signs of becoming an institutionalized emergency. It is malfunctioning not only for people of the Third World, the billions of poor, but for the small segment of humanity that belongs to what is called the First World, and it has been malfunctioning for over a decade.

In 1974 there was a United Nations Special Assembly on the New International Economic Order, which has become the substance of things hoped for but never seen, and it highlights the third crisis, the crisis of perception. Dr. Levitt mentioned this morning that our world has become multipolar, but there are two powers in particular that behave like Polyphemus, the cyclops with only one eye. They continue to see the world as bipolar and to interpret all phenomena accordingly.

This crisis of perception, looking at things with a myopic superpower vision, led to the mistake made by a certain power in 1983, the invasion of a Caribbean island. It is a mistake that continues to be made in estimating the importance of the Caribbean in the world scene. It is a mistake that has a very distinguished international thinker as one of its progenitors. I call him Henry the Second—Henry Kissinger—because by his own confession, Henry the First, Prince Klemens von Metternich, the chancellor of Austria in the nineteenth century, was his great mentor.

How have these crises affected the Caribbean? The debt crisis is showing up in the immense portion of national revenues that has to be paid by Caribbean countries, particularly Jamaica and Guyana, to service debts. The crises are showing up in the fact that these countries produce crops and other commodities that are at the mercy of the so-called free market, a volatile institution capable of rendering anything they produce unsalable in a short time. It is the sort of crisis that makes Caribbean countries lust after the tourist trade, knowing full well that, out of every dollar invested by tourists in the Caribbean, between 68 and 78 cents goes back to where the tourists came from.

Put these crises together and you have a kind of middle-aged crisis for the Caribbean independent countries. That middle-aged crisis reveals a fundamental division of outlook within the Caribbean, and it is that division of outlook I want to talk about.

I describe Caribbean thinkers, intellectuals, the intelligensia and ordinary people with two rather cumbersome terms: the *minimalists* and *maximalists*. A minimalist is one who agrees with the two superpowers in their interpretation of the international system. To a minimalist, the world is truly, fundamentally and irrevocably bipolar, and all other representations to the contrary are fictional and confused. The basic postulate of a minimalist, the starting point of his political life, is the hegemony of the United States in this hemisphere. Any good minimalist would say that is where Caribbean thinking starts. Seek first the kingdom of hegemony and all other things will be added unto you. They would say that that is political realism, and by political realism they mean survival politics. And they would say that to recognize the United States as the source of West Indian political reality is the fruitful way to proceed to live comfortably.

A maximalist starts with the postulate that the world is multipolar. A maximalist then proceeds to say that the Caribbean is not an insular extension of the United States, but a region possessing its own essence and identity, and that this essence and identity are characteristic of what is now called the South. To the maximalist, the Caribbean Sea is not an American lake. The Americans cannot use the old Latin phrase the Romans used for the Mediterranean—*mare nostrum*, "our sea." Maximalists would say that the Caribbean Sea is of one piece with the Bight of Benin, the Mozambique Channel, the Indian Ocean and the Gulf of Oman. It is extremely important to stop for a minute—because history has a way of shaping our perceptions, even when we forget that it is there—and to look briefly at how this division of visions came into being.

Minimalist thought is really a latter-day extension of British imperial thought. The reality of empire demanded that the West Indians see Britain as the hub of their universe, and themselves as outward and visible signs of the inner reality of British power. Their values were derivatively British, their tea at four o'clock in the afternoon was quintessentially British, their language was magnificently British. Because Britain is no longer the centre of the Pax Britannica, they have had to find another hub for their universe and so they have put a nearer power at the centre of that reality: the United States. They would say that small is not significant, however beautiful, and that West Indian geography is the geography of the United States, and there is where they would rest their visions.

Maximalists belong to a tradition that is extremely distinguished in its antecedents and prophets. West Indian maximalists include C.L.R. James, George Padmore, and my countryman and former pupil, Walter Rodney. It is a tradition of intellectual spaciousness at total variance with the size of the territories from which that spaciousness arises.

A long time ago, when Walter Rodney was fifteen and I was pretending to be teaching British Imperial History, I made a pact with the boys in his class that I would pass all of them in British Imperial History at the end of the year but would teach them West Indian history during the year. In the midst of a debate, Walter came out with a sentence with which I want to honour his memory tonight. And remember he was only fifteen. He said, "West Indian thinkers live more in time than in space." That is damn good for a fifteen year old, and he was right.

These miniscule territories, some of them, called by an historian, "crumbs of land floating on the bosom of the Caribbean," have been capable of a spaciousness that has amazed those who come from larger, landlocked entities deeply concerned with parochial responsibilities. But, in a very rare way, something the British did after emancipation set the stage for this spaciousness. Emancipation was the grand design in which Black West Indians would be liberated from the shackles of slavery and turned into Afro-Saxons—now a familiar phrase—and the brighter of them would be sent out to West Africa to make the Africans black Britishers. This was a very serious undertaking, and there is a long tradition of West Indians going out in the nineteenth century from Calibar College in Jamaica to Nigeria and teaching Nigerian tribesmen how to worship Jehovah in the strains of the English language. And the idea that West Indians would be spacious missionaries of the British Universal remained one of the traditions of British West Indian life.

Apart from that, West Indians never really lost their memories of Africa, however mythical. And this surfaces again and again in figures such as Marcus Garvey, who tried to make a link between Black Americans, West Indians and Africans way back in the 1930s and 1940s. It came up in George Padmore, Nkrumah's advisor, who saw the underpinnings of the new Marxist philosophy to be as broad as the expanses of the Atlantic Ocean that linked the Caribbean and West Africa, and called the connection Pan-Africanism. One of the most fascinating examples before Walter Rodney was C.L.R. James's book, *The Black Jacobins.*

C.L.R. James has been a Trotskyite throughout his intellectual life and he wrote *The Black Jacobins* in the 1930s to prove that the leaders of the Haitian revolution carried out the principles of Marxist revolution between 1793 and 1805, well in advance of *Das Kapital* or the *Communist Manifesto* or the birth of Lenin. He was showing that West Indians were well in advance in embodying the revolutionary principles that produced the Soviet Union and the other great revolutions of the world. Here is spaciousness for you, and that is a very peculiarly West Indian intellectual condition.

And Rodney! Rodney could not conceive of the history of West Africa as complete unless it were coupled with the history of the Caribbean. And he could not conceive of the history of the Caribbean as complete unless it were coupled with the history of Africa. That is why, as a Caribbean scholar, he did his thesis at the University of London on the history of Upper Volta. If he had lived, he would have written a history of Zimbabwe. He was that not uncommon Caribbean who is both a scholar and a political activist, so that at one and the same time he could be trying strenuously to bring down a government of a certain country, and at the same time writing a book about the evolution of the working class of that country.

The West Indies has had not only the womb of Africa, it has had the womb of India, and India for some has been a motherland that became a myth of perfection and, as that motherland gained political and international influence, so they gained political and ethnic pride.

Those things have made West Indian thinkers of the maximalist school global thinkers as well. They cannot conceive of imitating Washington or New York or Chicago. They conceive of the Caribbean Sea as a catalyst for changes taking place in a belt of the earth not belted by the United States.

For the minimalist, American power, America's sheer cultural ebullience and the pervasiveness of its images makes anything but the practice of capitalism in the Caribbean chimerical. For the minimalist, a capitalist economy ensures growth because it is basically a collusion between corporate investment and local enterprise.

Minimalists are usually populists and, if you will forgive a layman's definition of populism, it goes like this: the use of the power of the many by the few for the few. The minimalist would say that the way to redeem the working class from all the ills that they have become heir to is to co-opt them through trade-union structures and activities so, through co-option, the goodies of the system will trickle down to them.

Minimalists would say that the International Monetary Fund and the World Bank are gentler in their conditionalities on countries that practice private enterprise than on countries that practice either mixed economies or socialist ones, and the minimalist would add that it is in the arts and not in economics or in power play that West Indians can make small into beautiful and beautiful into significant.

On the other hand, the maximalist would take a view that structural transformation of West Indian society, with emphasis on greater self-reliance and local decision-making all through society, is the only way to conserve and build nations. Maximalists say that revolutions in perception are as important as revolutions in politics, and one basic revolution in perception is to see the Caribbean as a catalyst for the South in ideas and impulses. One thing maximalists are distinguished by is being active in trying to change the old international economic order into a new one, and they certainly support nonalignment, UNESCO, the Commonwealth,

UNCTAD. They would put it this way: You don't have to be a Marxist if you are not going to be a capitalist. You don't have to be a puppet of the Soviet Union if you are not going to be a puppet of the United States. If you're not going to be a banana republic, you don't have to be a balalaika republic either.

Through international institutions, maximalists would put active pressure on regimes such as South Africa to dismantle its system of apartheid, and on Rhodesia when it was in existence. Recall that Guyana as of 1970 and Jamaica as of 1975 gave part of their national budgets every year to African countries. They were the first countries outside Africa to do so, and they preceded even many African countries. That Caribbean sense of being astride the world is the mark of the maximalist and it is not surprising that the African, Caribbean and Pacific (ACP) group was actually conceived in the Caribbean.

The maximalist is interested in South-South co-operation; in taking technology from India and China; in mounting institutes of research which prevent the duplicating of scientific research among developing countries, which tend to constantly reinvent the wheel without knowing that it has been invented already elsewhere. He or she is deeply concerned that the nonaligned movement becomes not just a political instrument but a technological and economic instrument as well. There too global spaciousness is at work.

Grenada was a setback for the maximalist and an encouragement for the minimalist. A number of West Indians—we must not deny it—strongly favoured the invasion by the United States, so much so that one lady prime minister offered that it was at her instructions that the United States finally brought its marines onto the soil of Grenada. And part of the force was certainly made up of members from other Caribbean countries. We all thought Grenada would have killed the Caribbean Community (CARICOM), but CARICOM is not dead. We all thought the meeting of the heads of government that took place in the Bahamas would have had the quality of last rites. Instead, it had the quality of a stay of execution, if not of an active resurrection. It would seem that CARICOM has a recuperative power that has surprised everybody else. Having gone to the extreme of inviting external powers to regulate the politics of the region, those who did so, although not relenting, may be repining and, consequently, may want to keep CARICOM alive to prevent a repetition of that event.

It is at this point that Canada becomes important to my argument. Canada is the conquest of space by political will. It is the conquest of refractory distance by communication. It is taking a very ungainly piece of geography with all the polarities moving toward the south and then creating a confederation in which the institution of dispute becomes the substance of life. Certainly Canada has something, not necessarily aid, but political experience, to contribute to West Indians in their search for an expression of the regional unity already evident in the psychology of the maximalist but yet to be expressed in political structures.

I would like to see an institution to study the confederate, federal and collective behaviour of territories that have been nibbling at unity but never really bitten into it established in the Caribbean. And I would like to see that institute partly staffed by Canadians, whose daily experience is that of transcendent politics, if you will forgive the use of theological terms. Every Canadian is loyal, or partially so, to his municipality, then to his province and then to the federation. He disputes daily with each of them, but in doing so he keeps a kind of transcendental openness towards their functioning. As a result, Canada seems to have to negotiate its existence every week, but it has learnt the art superbly. Whether the Conservatives or the Liberals are in power, negotiation is an ongoing technique and that technique is part of the national woof and warp, the national welcome song.

One of the good things Canada can do that will have no strings will be to make available to us in the Caribbean, through presentations, sensitive interpretation and dialogue, the Canadian experience of weekly renegotiation of this difficult confederation of yours. It would help us to avoid fundamental errors that we might make at the beginning of an attempt at confederate existence. I would also add that not only should the Canadians do this, so should the Australians and so should some of the experts from India, which Galbraith in his mischievous wit described as a "functioning anarchy."

It is perfectly clear that some kind of collective entity is going to remain in the Caribbean. It is perfectly clear because the international economic and political situation is very abrasive. Even Jamaica, that Potemkin village of American enterprise in the Caribbean (you may remember that Prince Potemkin was Catherine the Great's lover, and she set him up to develop the Ukraine, and she visited once and he created a number of two-dimensional villages for her to pass through so she could see great progress in front and on the side, without seeing the middle), is discovering the hollowness of the development that comes through the trickle-down theory, by the presence of others who bring in money but do not seem to tap the reservoir of skill and will in the people.

Jamaica is discovering how evil it is not to try to be self-reliant. That is why its prime minister has probably decided not to kill CARICOM by withdrawing from it. If Jamaica is recognizing this point, so indeed will Dominica and so indeed will the rest. So CARICOM's survival is assured, which means a number of interesting things.

For one, it is now in the interest of Canada to promote regional integration, for that is where the centre of Canadian foreign policy lies. Canada quite rightly argues that a federal structure in the Caribbean would produce a meddlesomeness in political behaviour that will keep the meddlesomeness of the United States at bay.

Canada also sees that giving co-operative assistance (which last night was called aid) is much easier from federation to federation than bilaterally. The federation will have all the reserves of the central bank and a number of other collateral institutions with which to talk to the Canadians.

Most important of all, because Canada is a country that has made satellite communication an act of nationalism, one of the most potent forms of its existence, I think Canadian assistance will be at its acme in helping the West Indies to acquaint its people on the ground with the significance and the meaning of regions in the world of the 1980s. We can do that best through satellite, through communication systems that get right into the homes of people. If this happens, since the maximalists are the more articulate of the two groups, they will certainly dominate that system.

Canadian non-governmental organizations (NGOs) are part of the alternative Canadian imagination. In short, they take to the left what Canadian governments keep in the middle. Therefore, in learning self-reliance, in the business of research, in the business of establishing the essential importance of using local things, Canadian NGOs can be crucial and very useful in the Caribbean. Because NGOs are usually small and relate people to people even when they're talking about nuts and bolts, this will help to diminish what I call the confluence of maximals, whereby governments demand enormous airports and the government of Canada accedes for propaganda purposes.

Canada is a country bounded on the north by mystery, on the south by hegemony, on the east by history and on the west by the East. The West Indies is a region bounded on the north by assertion, on the west by volatility, on the south by debts and on the east by the South. Canada and the Caribbean have one thing in common: hegemony and assertiveness are both their neighbours. They therefore can start from there. We both live in uncomfortable proximity to a superpower but, more than that, we are both peoples who take history seriously, we are both peoples who are always looking for alternatives to the breathing presence near us. That is a starting point. Not so much large subventions of massive aid but large subventions of historical understanding and historical imagination are called for. If Canada cannot rise to the occasion, we West Indian maximalists will make it do so.

Michael Manley: *Caribbean Development in Historical Perspective*

(Michael Manley, M.P., is a former prime minister of Jamaica; the text of this speech can also be found in a companion volume to this publication, *Rethinking Caribbean Development*)

I would like to share my view of the way our understanding of development has evolved in the last thirty to forty years. I think it is always important when one is doing something of this sort to confess one's own ideological position. I speak from within the experience of a plural democratic society in the Third World struggling to make sense and meaning of its independence, and I also speak from within the ideology of democratic socialism.

I would like to trace how I think people responsible within the political process in Caribbean countries and other parts of the Third World have understood development as a process, and to trace the evolution of that understanding. One has to begin here if one is to make sense of the mess that we are in today and the question of where we can go from here.

The Puerto Rican Model and the Evolution of Development Ideas in Jamaica
Development was first thought about, in a sense, after World War II—it has been about a forty-year experience. In plural democracies, development was seen first of all as an economic process, as if that was self-contained, which, it was hoped, would lead to social change as something that could be seen by itself, and to an improvement in the quality of life, as if quality of life were an abstract consequence of certain economic changes making certain social changes possible. The political process was understood as nothing more than the facilitator of these things. Therefore, right at the beginning of ideas about development in Third World countries, there was a fatal separation of the concepts of economic activity, social consequences and how the two interact to produce a quality of life.

The Puerto Rican model reflected the idea that development must be led by industrialization, that those broad, deformed agricultural societies that had been bitten by colonialism within the imperialist framework had to be transformed by industrialization. Because there was no means of internal capital accumulation to accomplish industrialization, it was to be achieved by foreign capital within the framework of free market mechanisms. The trick was to find a way to attract foreign capital to do all the jobs that had to be done.

Those who were responsible for the political situation saw themselves as setting the rules; providing the incentives, such as ten-year tax holidays, that would attract foreign capital; and waging a discreet war with trade union movements, because the secret of the seduction of foreign capital was the wage differential. If the wage versus productivity differential in Third

World countries was more favourable than it was in developed countries, there would be an incentive for foreign capital to move. Therefore, a discreet and sometimes indiscreet purpose of government was to manipulate the trade union movement so it would not, by its pressure to increase wages, destroy this incentive. All of this was regarded as a separated, remote regulatory function. It was assumed that development would result from other processes that would be set in motion.

In Jamaica, for example, development was associated with internal industrial activity generated by import substitution—we would now import raw materials to make Colgate-Palmolive toothpaste instead of importing the entire tube of toothpaste. There was a tendency to ignore agriculture, which, in most cases, fell into decline.

Let us test theory against practice by using the case of Jamaica, the case I know most intimately. Between 1962, when Jamaica became independent, and 1972, when a first phase of its independent history came to an end, there was absolute reliance on the Puerto Rican model in the approach to development, and this model was associated with spectacular results in the classic indicators then accepted as measures of development: economic aggregate indicators. Between 1962 and 1972, Jamaica maintained the astonishing rate of 6 percent per annum growth in gross national product (GNP), which must have been very nearly as good as anywhere else in the world. By the end of this period, those figures reflected an over $1,000 per capital GNP which means we had moved into a middle range—again according to the classic aggregate indicators. If one looked at those indicators, one would think, my God, this is one of the success stories of the twentieth century.

Let us now test the indicators against the experience. While the GNP was growing at 6 percent per annum, unemployment grew from 12 percent in 1962 to 25 percent ten years later. The rich versus poor dichotomy that had been a social tragedy of our long colonial history was not improving but had grown worse. There had been no significant improvements in health or education services. After ten years of growth, only 16 percent of all children over the age of fifteen ever received one day of instruction in anything thereafter, even as an apprentice in a factory. The system was growing like mad, creating a richer and richer crust of people within the foreign capital growth pattern and quietly destroying almost every child by total neglect after the age of fifteen. I won't even bother to dwell on the 40 percent illiteracy.

Economic growth did take place but did not lead to social change, and there was an actual deterioration in the quality of life. At the upper level of society, corrupt consumerist values were growing; at the lower level, alienation was mounting. There was this paradox: even as Jamaica was trying to use its independence as an opportunity to correct its historical disabilities, its economy was growing more and more dependent because the engine of growth was entirely foreign. Even limited efforts at internal growth through import substitution were locking it into industries that depended heavily on raw materials from abroad. Increased structural, capital and technological dependence created no social change but did bring a deterioration in the quality of life, both psychologically and materially.

It is not surprising that some had second thoughts. These second thoughts had no doubt been present all along in the minds of the intellectuals, but what an intellectual understands takes a little more time to penetrate the thicker skull of a political activist like myself—or perhaps we're distracted, distracted by pressure. During the second half of the sixties, a second wave of thinking began among political leaders. Two critical understandings were being identified. One was the understanding of the problem of structural dependence, that is, in an independent national economic framework you have to address the consequences of deep structural dependence of the kind that had been planted by the long colonial experience. The second was the understanding of linkage theory, the understanding that one has to do two critical things to build a viable economy: link agriculture and industry, and link raw materials and processing.

This was a tremendous movement forward in thought. Once one understands the structural and linkage aspects of economic development, one is commanded to attend to agricultural development as a foundation for industrial development, and that gets one into the whole agribusiness concept. Knowing that raw material processing reduces external dependence forces one to attempt to maximize activity internally and create a logical relationship between the two things.

Caribbean people remember the tremendous role played by thinkers, such as Willie Demas, formerly of the Caribbean Community (CARICOM), and Allister MacIntyre, both of whom began to sensitize Caribbean people to structural and linkage ideas. A fundamental qualification of the Puerto Rican model was introduced. The state cannot invite foreign capital to resolve the problem of structural dependence because that would be a contradiction. The state cannot invite foreign capital to deal with internal linkage because this involves strategic investment for the country's own economic development, which may not be profitable or attractive to foreign capital anyway.

So, the response within the plural democracies was that the state had to be seen as more than a by-standing regulator. The state had to become involved in planning. It had to become involved in the question of internal accumulation at whatever price, because without internal accumulation, you cannot develop. It had to become involved in the reorientation of skills, the conscious use of education and everything else to develop the capacities within society to tackle those things that cannot be done for us by foreign capital. Most importantly, the state had to become the creator of institutions, institutions to manage agricultural development of certain kinds and so on. The state would be an intervenor and innovator rather than merely a regulator.

Now if this seems like an apology for socialist ideas, forgive me. Objective experience is compelling you to attend to what are in fact socialist ideas, but I am not imposing them upon you from the presumptions of theory. I am trying to indicate that even if you were not a socialist, your common sense would force you to these understandings and this kind of activity if you were concerned with nationally directed development.

This second wave of thinking was still incomplete in its understanding of the influence of the international environment and contained very little understanding of the role of the political process.

A third wave of thought began during the 1970s. Again these concepts may have already been understood by intellectuals. But now activists were beginning to understand the significance of the external environment. In trade, for example, a basis for internal accumulation is destroyed if your tractors are costing more and more and you are getting less for your sugar or whatever it may be. Our terms of trade historically have acted as a transfer of wealth and accumulated capacity that has worked its misery on generations.

Activists also were beginning to have to come to terms with the dominant reality of today's world, which is the transnationalization of production and finance. Briefly, the present international financial system was set in place at Bretton Woods forty years ago. The International Monetary Fund (IMF) operates to maintain the dominating power of transnational corporations by insisting that countries control basic production and finance in the world. So, one might have the most intelligent understanding of development problems, structure, linkage and so on, only to find that the external environment was operating to defeat nationally-directed development.

This discovery led to the formulation of the prescriptions of the new international economic order, which are practical proposals for significant change that sometimes are obscured in the rhetorical-sounding term, *New International Economic Order*. I beg you not to be disturbed by the rhetoric implied in the name but to understand the specifics about trade, finance and so on that are the guts of what is proposed. It also led to the development of "South thinking," the understanding of the importance of Third World countries working in co-operation and collaboration with other Third World countries to build incremental productive capacity through their own giant efforts rather than by dependence on the multinational co-operation system.

Two new ideas became important. One was the idea of diversification. Along with attempts to change the way the economic structure works in the world, one has to diversify links with that outside world so as to reduce dependence on particular sources of capital, production and trade. So the second important idea was what we call "delinkage theory," which recognizes the importance of slowly delinking aspects of the Third World economy to ease the crippling dependency syndrome.

This has been a quick look at how I think development ideas have evolved under the pressure of events. Now I will illustrate the theory we practice. I think we understand the things I indicated: the importance of structural change, delinkage, the international environment and so on. We also know that one cannot move towards development if one regards economic and social change as separate phenomena which happen in sequence—they have to be parts of a single process.

These ideas, held by our party, the People's National Party (PNP), were important within the plural democratic framework of Jamaica of the 1970s because we understood that social change must be a part of the transformation of economic development. If you do not have education or health, who is going to do it, unless it's just a lot of foreign people who come and do it for us, however nice they may be. Also, if you are going to overcome the tremendous problems of development, the people must feel something moving in their lives and not merely know that a few more people punch a clock at starvation wages in the hope that their children may go to school. The going to school and the hope and the experience must all be part of punching clocks.

When we look back at that period, we made tremendous mistakes, but there were some real achievements. Certainly our educational system began to mobilize to provide skills, and there were tremendous changes in education, qualitatively and quantitatively. We did significant things in services and law, and moved the society towards justice, with women's rights, workers' rights and so on. We created institutions for agribusiness development. We established linkages within the economy between raw materials and processing. Vigorous land reform was carried out. Attention was focused on domestic agriculture and this sector grew at 8 percent per annum for eight consecutive years.

We were active in the broad strategy of the new international economic order and played an active part in South-South co-operation. We played a positive role, with faith and commitment, in the formation of CARICOM, to provide a political umbrella for economic co-operation. We began to build bridges between the English-speaking Caribbean and the Latin American Caribbean, because we saw no reason why Spanish and British imperial history should leave an irrelevant division in the experience of what is one region.

There are many ways in which the Latin American Caribbean and the English-speaking Caribbean can co-operate practically. If the English-speaking Caribbean cannot start a shipping service, it can use those of Venezuela, Mexico or Cuba instead of relying on a multinational corporation. There were opportunities to explore aluminum development with

Mexican flare-up gas and Jamaican aluminum—neither country could accomplish this on its own.

When I grew up, the thought of an English-speaking Caribbean country co-operating with a Spanish-speaking Caribbean country was quite unthinkable. It has taken us a long time to recover from propaganda from the days when Drake beat the Spaniards and Nelson beat up everybody else. This propaganda implanted an assumption of inherent superiority among English-speaking Caribbean people. This amuses me, looking back on it. Neither Drake nor Nelson was black, but my black Caribbean brothers will attest that we all grew up thinking Spanish-speaking people were not as good as us. Very funny, but part of history and one has to beat it down.

In spite of the things the PNP did, which I think were right and strategically focused, it all ended up in political disaster. As we addressed social change in Jamaica, the local elite took off with their money for Miami and later Toronto. Our attempt to build regional co-operation, which had to include Cuba because Cuba is part of the region, led to U.S. hostility. In time it was all over within our vigorous plural democracy and we were blown away for the time being. The GNP sank badly over the eight years and, eventually, in a wave of violence, destabilization and other kinds of confusion, we were defeated. Although we were trying to approach development through a deeper understanding of its requirements, in that plural democracy we were unable to develop a political process that could keep it together and keep it moving.

The Cuban and Tanzanian Models
I've always understood two ideas. First, it is idle to imitate. I don't mean that one should reinvent the wheel, but every society must understand its own dynamics and the nature of its own political process and not delude itself by trying to imitate what has been achieved somewhere else in different circumstances. There may be similarities and commonalities but, in the end, one has to explore reality within the dynamics of one's own situation. That is why I work within a plural democracy. That is the framework within which I work now and will work for the rest of my active life. That is the reality.

Second, it is stupid to ignore. It is stupid to ignore things that can be indicative if you open your mind. When I think of the present, almost catastrophic situation in Central America and the Caribbean, two striking examples of development come to mind: Cuba and Tanzania. Again, I want to make it clear that I'm not advocating the stupid idea that any country should try to duplicate these unique situations, which followed their own internal logic, but I would like to look at the lessons that can be learned.

What is interesting about Cuba is that it has gone through extraordinary lurches and reversals of economic and development strategies. Cuba started out with a rapid liquidation of the capitalist system, and it then had to endure a massive flight of skills. It then got into a tremendous internal controversy involving two theories of socialist development: one was Guevarist and essentially idealistic-romantic and the other was Soviet and very pragmatic. During a marvellous period in their history, the Cubans ran both systems, one under Ernesto (Ché) Guevara and the other under Carlos Rodriguez. They endured the isolation of embargo. In the end they had to transfer an element of dependence from the United States to USSR. They really wanted to pursue a consistent economic, social and political strategy after 1971.

The extraordinary coherence and achievements of the Cuban revolution are undeniable today. Production is beginning to move and there have been great achievements in education, health, hospital services and so on. When one looks at the Cuban revolution—which one may like or dislike, that's one's own business—one has to admit that it is a reality, that it is established and that it represents a triumph of its political process. It endured through many changes because it found an internal political process that mobilized it and gave it coherence and effectiveness, in terms that were valid to the great majority of its people. So, Cuba is a success story, given the objective realities of the international environment, that was born clearly of a political process.

Tanzania interests me because it is just the opposite. It is now common to describe the Tanzania and Julius Nyerere model as a failure because the country's per capita income is still only $285 per annum, it still has only one doctor to every 17,000 people, it has numerous problems related to poverty and so on. Although Tanzania has had very real social successes, nonetheless the catholic approach is to call it a failure, a failed model, because it is in difficulty with the IMF and has not achieved a significant acceleration in its economic base to improve the life of the Tanzanian people. One could talk about its tremendous vulnerability in terms of trade, the tremendous effect of drought, the tremendous effect of being a front-line country and leader in the struggle against South Africa, and the catastrophic effect of the war to remove the bloody Ugandan tyrant Amin, but those topics might be dismissed as apologies. What interests me is that the Tanzanian people had an opportunity in 1983 to address this question. Should we go the route that the IMF is pressuring us to go and get additional foreign exchange and foreign capital and therefore an easement in the immediate shortage of capital and financing, or should we refuse to pay the price that that would require and continue, however tough the road may be, on our egalitarian ujamaa-socialist path, with the great financial disabilities that that path implies?

This election in Tanzania under its one-party system was fascinating to me. Tanzania has vigorous elective processes and candidates run and have points of view but, for the first time, there was what nearly amounted to a two-party election within the single framework of the Chama Cha

Mapinduzi (CCM). On one side were the pragmatists and economists who felt the country was getting nowhere, that the GNP was not growing and so on, who campaigned for acceptance of the IMF approach to development. On the other side were the young idealists, or whatever you want to call them, who argued, let us build our kind of socialism as we understand it, let us follow that stable course even if the road is tough.

There was a massive victory for the ujamaa-socialists over the pragmatists in a perfectly free election. This showed that somewhere in the Tanzanian development model is a political process able to be consistent and hold the people to a course of action which they understand and find valid in their experience. This process has altered what has been described as a failure. This is the inside story you don't read about in the *New York Times*.

Development Models for the Future

May I remind you that the external debt in Central America moved from $5.9 billion in 1978 to $13.8 billion in 1982, an increase of 173 percent. By 1986, South Korea will have an external debt of $65 billion, a figure slightly larger than its gross national product.

If we look at Jamaica, after we were ejected from office, that really describes what happened. It may happen in due course to those who ejected us. In fact, it will happen. It's just a matter of when. When we left office in Jamaica, I was deeply worried about the fact that with a gross national product of $2.5 billion, we had an external debt of $1.2 billion. I really remember that—it was blowing my mind as the then prime minister, God help me. In the four years we have been out of office, the external debt has grown to $3.4 billion. Jamaica is now in the stupefying position of having an external debt that is worth about a year and one half of its GNP. I mean the thing is like *Alice in Wonderland*. Our gross export earnings, including tourism, are $800 million, and just to service debt this year will cost $600 million—75 percent of the gross foreign-exchange receipts. Oil costs another $300 million. So any way one takes it, one has to borrow money to pay interest, but I defy anyone to run his home or business that way. Where it's going to end, God only knows.

The historian Roxborough has suggested that *development* can be defined as *an increase in the capacity for controlled transformation of the social structure.* After years of experience, I would like to suggest that in looking at development one should consider (1) the capacity of the social group to agree on roles, which is the political process; (2) the capacity of the group to create the institutions through which goals may be realized, which is the social process; and (3) the development of productive forces to make material well-being available to all, which is the economic process. I deliberately put it in that order: political first, social second and economic third, because I think the fundamental fallacy of the early thinking was that it put the whole thing the wrong way around. Economics may determine the quality of life, but if you want to change economics, only the political process can direct that change. Finally, one should consider (4) how, through the interaction of all those things, an environment can be created in which people can realize their potential for self-expression, self-realization and democratic participation. I have learned important facts about the role of a country's internal dimensions and the role of external co-operation in development. I assume that the international environment will not quickly change. I can't base policy on the hope that somebody may persuade Ronald Reagan to have a change of heart. I'm going to assume that while he is in office Washington will be hostile to any kind of change, and that that hostility may even continue after his presidency.

What can Canada do, how could Canada focus its action nationally and internationally in a way that can help? One of the paradoxes we deal with in plural democracies is that competitive populism is the main enemy of development. The plural democratic system has a terrible tendency to trivialize politics, and a terrible capacity to make people vulnerable to manipulation internally and externally. It can deliver working-class people into a form of manipulation, internally and externally. If competing parties only promise a better life but do not direct attention to the mobilization, disciplined effort, and other things necessary to bring about that better life, then it becomes impossible for the people to do what they have to do to save themselves.

Effective economic strategy includes reducing dependence on the outside. One cannot direct development if one does not control this dependence. One hero of American civilization was Alexander Hamilton. He was a bright guy who came from the Caribbean. People rarely talk these days about the period after the American Revolution when a genuine bourgeois revolution occurred in the USA to protect its capitalist productive forces. Alexander Hamilton enunciated this policy to the outside world: foreign capital, hands off. The Americans did not allow foreign capital near their civilization for generations and made sure that their vast national opportunity was an opportunity for local development and local capital formation. Now they are the very ones who turn around to tell the rest of the world that only American capital can save them. Well, I'm not buying it. We may need foreign capital up to a point, but it cannot be the agent of our salvation. So delinkage with the outside is critical. The internal linkage of the economy is vital. A methodology that defines the ways to increase the internal accumulation of capital is fundamental. Diversification is a part of that, and social transformation has to walk hand in hand with all these things. The critical points I want to convey are that all of this must happen together and that all must be a part of, and not the result of, the political process.

Let me illustrate these points. As we would agree, internal investment is indispensable. In a poor country, internal investment can only be achieved at the price of sacrifice because poor countries don't have significant surpluses to exploit for that purpose. If there is to be sacrifice, it must be shared sacrifice. One cannot ask Jamaicans to sacrifice the standards of the poor for capital accumulation when the poor are already on the verge of starvation. So the society has to be capable of sharing sacrifice so accumulated capital can be used. If it is to be shared, sacrifice must be understood and felt to be justified. If patience is required, then people must simultaneously experience an improvement in their lives that is valid to them. If any of its conditions are missing, this improvement cannot happen; and if it cannot happen, forget development. Let's all become neocolonies and client states for the rest of history.

Development will only happen if it is the result of people participating in the process by which they formulate the problem, formulate a solution, understand the means and commit themselves to what is necessary. Therefore, my belief is that Third World development has to begin with the understanding that politics needs to be redefined and understood anew. Politics must become developmental and be participatory at all levels. I say participatory because unless the people mobilize themselves to address the fundamental problems, rather than relying on the heckling and lectures of strident politicians, they will never commit themselves to what is needed, nor will they understand what to do if politics is not developmental—meaning involved in raising consciousness and understanding.

In our party, God help us, I don't know what. It's a race with time, but we now devote tremendous time and effort to holding serious political education classes that study history and how economies are formed, so as to acquire an understanding of what the development process is all about. This is completely different from the conventional wisdom of plural politics which is, let us, a group of elite, sit down in a room and work out a nice-sounding plan in which everybody is going to get a house and a garage. Actually, in Jamaica we don't even aspire that far, but someday somebody is going to come up with a plan promising Jamaicans garages or at least kennels for bicycles or something. This approach is remote and promissory; it does not involve the people in anything except the conditions of their own frustration and defeat later on when what was promised does not happen. If we cannot reverse that, forget development. How can we build domestic agriculture if our middle class believes it will surely rot if it can't buy tinned mushrooms from abroad?

Within traditional, externally directed economic development, the union movement very often, without thinking about it, tends to join with the employing classes in the youth of economic opportunity to generate higher profits and higher wages, while actually depressing the standards of the already poor—not because they mean to do so but because that's how the system works if it is not founded on an understanding of national priorities. I am a unionist to my backbone, but I am very concerned that we understand how the union movement can accidentally become an agent in the growing rich versus poor disparity in Third World societies.

All this is related to South-South co-operation. In the Caribbean, CARI-COM is off to a very fine start but it will be historically meaningless if it does not become the vehicle of an economic integration process. Eric Williams' idea was to form a Caribbean food corporation using land skills in Jamaica and products from the Trinidadian industry for fertilizers. That is the kind of thing the Caribbean needs. Jamaica alone and Trinidad alone do not have the skills nor are they large enough to be as effective in development alone as they would be if they built their productive forces through co-operation. If we do not do it by co-operation, we will be driven by the pressure of foreign exchange to depend more and more on the multinational corporations to do it for us, which would merely repeat the cycle all over again.

What can Canada do? Canada can be a voice in the struggle for a new international economic order. Right now the greatest need is to deal with the IMF.

Louis Wiltshire: *CARICOM and Regional Co-operation in the Caribbean*

(Louis Wiltshire is the deputy director of CARICOM, Guyana)

This is my first visit to Halifax and I'm glad that I have been able to come. As someone who once studied history, I am aware that there have been long-standing connections between Atlantic Canada and the Caribbean, connections which have fallen to some extent into disuse. There are many connections, but over time people have perhaps drifted in different directions, and so it is very useful for us to take the opportunity of this unique conference to reconsider the directions in which both our areas are going and the extent to which we can bring them together in co-operation.

I have served internationally for many years, and in diplomacy for many more years, and I'm committed to co-operative action. From the perspective of the Caribbean, this is perhaps not surprising. We have some 5 million people scattered across thirteen countries. Coming up on the plane, I was reading about a recent budget in one of the less-developed countries. It was some EC$97 million of expenditure; and EC$99 million of revenue, approximately US$35 million. Not an enormous sum of money. A small territory with just a few thousand people, but it's so well managed that it pays its dues regularly. However, all our territories suffer from the familiar ailments of underdevelopment: short human resources, short financial resources. We are passing through a period of acute economic stringency that emphasizes our ailments, but that's the norm for our countries. We are, by and large—with the possible exception of Trinidad and Tobago, which has had the benefit of oil over the past few years—all poor. So, despite the fact that we have taken advantage of decolonization and assumed our independence, we can't do all the things that traditionally have been assumed to be the activities of independent nation-states.

We do not have large markets, we do not have large production bases, so poverty is endemic. Acting alone, we are bound to look insignificant not only on the world scene but on the regional scene and, more importantly, we are unable to be masters of our own affairs, with possibly disastrous consequences. We had in the Caribbean just recently an example of what can happen when a power from outside the region decides something is important to it and takes action, regardless of what the people in the region might feel. In that particular instance, some people were happy perhaps, but the point is they did not really have a choice.

I am not suggesting that any combination of forces and resources in the Caribbean could create an entity that could withstand the USA. That is virtually impossible. But there is a possibility of a more effective economic and social existence in the Caribbean together, better than if we attempt to go it alone.

We all have radios and televisions. We are all now plugged into the American communications media, and we consequently have the same expectations of the good life as people in the Western world, but without the resources to support it. This combination is a recipe for social upheaval and political disorder. One can't expect people to be tranquil if they don't have jobs, if their children aren't getting educated, if they see no prospect for a future amelioration of the situation.

It is in this situation that CARICOM exists and was brought into existence—in the perception that individually we are not capable of doing very much and the only real chance we have is to try to do it together. There is an illustrious history of precedents behind it, including the University of the West Indies which antedated even the Federation of the West Indies itself, which failed, and then CARIFTA, the free trade area—and now the Caribbean Community and Common Market, which many people say is failing or has failed. They are amazed that it has not been buried, but having gone there just a few months ago, and after careful inquiry as to whether I was going to help bury the corpse or whether there was in fact a living future, I am convinced that it is far from dead. Having attended a series of ministerial meetings and the latest conference of heads of government in Nassau in July, I am convinced that the political leaders of the Caribbean, all of them, regard the integration movement as vital to their national interests. Whether or not it might from time to time be politic to do so, they support it on a day to day basis and continue to give it additional mandates to do things they cannot do themselves or which they want supported effectively in the way they have come to know, as the technicians in the Secretariat and in the countries of CARICOM who co-operate with the Secretariat will be able to do.

CARICOM has three basic mandates. One is economic integration—this is rather well known. The second is functional co-operation in areas such as education and health. And the third is co-ordination of foreign policy. This is the tricky area, because foreign policy is to many people the most important manifestation of sovereign independence. Anyone who attempts to superimpose a decision-making process from outside the individual sovereignty runs the risk of being seen as supranational and as threatening the continued existence of that individual independence and sovereignty. Despite that, we had in New York a few weeks ago an informal consultation of CARICOM foreign ministers attending the General Assembly. We had excellent attendance and discussed a host of issues connected with the General Assembly. Out of that discussion came the repeated assertion that these things must be co-ordinated through CARICOM, that information on these things must be circulated among the states and to CARICOM for it to circulate to the states, because people found, examining some of these issues (e.g., the issue of candidacies to various international bodies), that there was often no central grasp by the individual state of what was being done by many different branches.

Our countries participate in health matters through the World Health Organization (WHO) and the Pan American Health Organization (PAHO) and in other matters through the UN Educational, Scientific and Cultural Organization (UNESCO), the International Labour Organization (ILO), the UN Industrial Development Organization (UNIDO) and other international agencies. And in all of them we have entities within the countries which do the direct relating. As one foreign minister said, when we go to a technical meeting and political issues arise, if we don't have foreign-affairs personnel there, the people from the technical ministries are caught off balance. They do not know the background, the foreign-policy considerations that have gone into the formation of their government's position, and sometimes they don't even know what their government's position is. So they have a dilemma: to function, they have to go to health meetings, labour meetings, industrial minister's meetings and so on, but because of the general background and the shortage of money and resources, they cannot always send foreign-policy specialists along with the industrialization people. Here again the ministers saw a role for CARICOM. I asked one foreign minister whether he would support the increased staff required. He said, it's infinitely cheaper to do it through CARICOM than for all thirteen of us to try to do it by ourselves.

There are several instances in practice of that. We are currently engaged in negotiations with the European Community for a follow-up of Lomé. And again and again the Caribbean ministers and Brussels and the industry ministers who tend to go there have insisted that the CARICOM Secretariat must provide the technical backstopping for that—we must not merely prepare the technical briefing papers but we must send staff to serve as technical advisors during the negotiations. We have on occasion demurred because it is extremely costly and they have not given us any more money to do it. Everything, of course, has to be resolved. These practical instances convince us of the value of the integration movement, of acquired expertise in one central place, which is found by its political constituency to be of irreplaceable value.

The integration movement does not have good press, and that's important because most of its work is secret. Every document coming out of every meeting is confidential, restricted. They have decided recently on a process of derestriction, but that is for documents many years old. Anything going to meeting now is unlikely to be made publicly available for at least five years. Ministers, to avoid immediate political trouble, have specified that what they have discussed and decided should be kept secret.

However, I can tell you of various decisions because they have progressed. We had a mandate to find a way to stimulate trade, which was in the doldrums in the last two years. During these two years a huge number of people have discovered that the abstract entity called CARICOM affected them, because factories were producing goods to trade under the CARICOM trading regime, and if that did not work, then those jobs were being lost because the factories were closing in many countries. We launched an investigation to find out who was producing what and to discern the facts of the trading situation over the past few years.

There was an extraordinary meeting of the Common Market Council of Ministers in Antigua in June 1984, and they came up with a package of proposals in which they identified industries which had the productive capacity to supply the regional market to an extent that would made a difference in the trading figures and the economic picture. Now, that's clearly not all industries, so we decided that that list should be secret. It would be a little awkward for the Secretariat to do detailed work on an industry while keeping secret the fact that that industry was one of those being focused on. The list was subsequently published after the conference of heads of government had considered, modified and ratified it. The concern, even though there was extensive media attention on the extraordinary session of the Common Market Council, was the restimulation of trade and sometimes it looked as if they were hiding another failure. That is an extreme case.

We in the Secretariat have tended to be like civil servants and to keep our own perceptions to ourselves, to let the political leaders speak. We have tended to assume that our vision of reality as we see it can be taken for granted and must be shared by all right-thinking people, and of course this is not so. If you do not tell others, they do not know. For example, when I went into CARICOM in January 1984, I said that trade was essential, without it CARICOM would not survive. However, the perception that CARICOM is failing can only exist because people are not thinking about the other, noncontroversial things that are taking place. Our ministers of education have met and discussed technical and vocational education, improvement of reading skills, and they have discussed the Caribbean Examinations Council (CEC) with its host of problems. They have discussed education and a series of things that are important to large numbers of people in our communities.

Education, for example, is fundamental in the Caribbean. Most of us from the Caribbean are here at this conference because our parents and our societies put an emphasis on education and we are the beneficiaries, and that is taken for granted. However, if co-operation in education, whether through CEC or the universities all agreeing on common standards in nursing education or whatever, were to collapse, our individual countries would be unable to do all of those things on their own, and the deterioration which would take place would affect people as surely as the loss of jobs would. This is not something people think through on a regular basis, but the fact is that ministers of education and permanent secretaries of education meet, agree on and mandate a host of things.

For example, they mandated that a task force should meet on technical and vocational education and come up with a program for meaningful advance in that area, because it is obviously critical to the future. A task force met in St. Lucia some three weeks ago and decided that the timetable was unrealistic, that it could not report to the ministers before December as mandated. They stretched it into March and said that it should be ongoing. They could not pool together in a few months all the proposals which one hundred sources have been making, UNIDO, all the work in the vocational schools, and come up with a regional program that takes the thing forward significantly. Here the ministers had launched something they considered fundamental and urgent, and there was to be no word of it in any media coverage anywhere in the Caribbean or outside. It is not necessarily the fault of the media. We have not launched a public information campaign on that subject and it is partly our fault.

I want to tell you today that in the area of functional co-operation, which to me is absolutely vital as a constituent element of the integration movement, work is going on that is as important as anything taking place in the field of trade. I have indicated as well that in co-ordination of foreign policy, we also have work going on—whether it is the spectacular kind of work from which we expect results quickly as in the Lomé negotiations (however disappointing on the global level those might be in the levels of resources being spoken about) or work in other areas, for example, where the Caribbean decides that if it has twelve votes from twelve independent members in the United Nations, that the effect of those votes can be maximized by consulting in advance and co-ordinating positions.

CARICOM has a staff of some 200 people—some 80 professionals and other support staff. We have a budget of approximately US$5 million, including project funds for specific activities. We are what I call a validating agency to many technical assistance donors for requests coming out of the Caribbean. It is a slightly ambivalent role we have to play there. The Fund for Technical Cooperation, for example, will cable us and say, do you agree, do you certify that this activity for which we have a request for funding from X agency or body is genuinely a priority for the region? (And we have had to tell some of our staff members that the fact that they might wish to make a request in the same general area subsequently is no ground for holding back, delaying or anything like that.) Because we pool together so many currents of opinion, we have so many opportunities for seeing policy formed. People assume that we can give an accurate estimate of what is a priority and what is not in a situation, externally and internally, of very scarce resources. But that too is a side benefit of the integration movement, because otherwise we would have, as we still do to some extent, a very disorganized situation in which people are going to the same donors or sponsors for competing projects without anybody taking a look at what the region really needs. The problem is to find out what the region feels to be the priority in this area for funding. What will make the greatest impact collectively over time? And we were the central people ultimately, along with the UN Commission for Latin America (ECLA) and the Organisation of Eastern Caribbean States (OECS) secretariat in the smaller territories, and it is a function which increasingly has to be done by the integration movement in its various phases.

Some people, for example, have seen the development of the OECS as a threat to the overall Caribbean integration movement, and in that regard I would like to tell a small story, which caught us by surprise, from the heads of government meeting. Many of you may remember that there was an initiative there for the exploration of the possibility of a CARICOM Olympic team in the future. And we in the Secretariat put down for the heads that we would explore this in consultation with the OECS secretariat. Now we thought we were playing it safe by developing a sports desk and so on, and the OECS prime minister snapped at us. This is a CARICOM initiative. Why are you trying to divide us? Now, we had never ceased consultation with the OECS secretariat, who are our friends, but the perception that separating them out could be something harmful, something we should avoid doing on certain occasions, came through very clearly, and we realized this is a much more complicated thing than we had assumed. The OECS members themselves see CARICOM as an entity in which they participate and see their co-ordination and consultation in OECS as something separate and nonthreatening to its activities. This is just to underline the problem we have had, in the integration movement, of perceptions which can lead us into feeling that things are not happening or are not happening effectively.

I come back to the question of communications because all leaders do not articulate their perceptions and because those of us who serve the movement as secretariats are not ourselves taking the time to articulate our perceptions of the priorities and strengths as they develop over time—perhaps we do in meetings which are not public—and to convey to the public the various ways in which the integration movement is affecting it. Now I mentioned to Mr. Emery Fanjoy that transportation was a critical area of concern for us. We are going to have a meeting of ministers of transportation in another few weeks. We have a mandate currently to explore passenger shipping in the Caribbean, and we are looking for funding. But there is no easy way for the people of the region to move about, and of course there are barriers to freedom of movement to persons in the Caribbean. Here is one area where we have traditionally been linked with Atlantic Canada. Here is an area where it is absolutely essential we do something concrete and positive, but it is not in the forefront of people's consciousness as an issue to be dealt with by the integration movement. It is not in the forefront of anybody's discussion as a possible area of co-operation between Atlantic Canada and the Caribbean, but it is merely one of many, which if we use the opportunity of meetings such as this, we can identify for constructive follow-up.

Jean Augustine: *Third World Canadians and the Question of Development*

(Jean Augustine is with the Canadian Advisory Council on the Status of Women and the Congress of Black Women of Canada)

Twenty-four years ago, coming to Toronto from Grenada, I had a real difficulty explaining to people where I came from. I can think of several serviettes, bits of paper and whatnot on which I drew a map of the Caribbean to show where Grenada was. In 1984 I do not have to do that. Everyone now can pronounce the word *Grenada*, and I think everyone knows where it is. So out of every situation comes something positive.

I come from Grenada, and it is said that one is shaped by one's past experiences. What I want to do is share four little stories with you, and I want you to keep these stories in mind. At the end I will come back to these four stories and make a link.

The first story: A man and wife just returned from the Caribbean with tapes and slides and everything. They had a really good time there and they did a lot of work. A number of us sat through the presentation and as we were leaving the hall, it was raining. We were standing at the front of this church waiting for the shower to be over when the man who had made the presentation came up to another friend and myself standing together, two black faces in a sea of Canadian faces, and said to us, we have to find a babysitter and a housekeeper. Why does that story remain in my mind?

The second story has to do with a group of women who asked us to meet with them to do a little mediating. That is, could we talk about our situation, listen and comment. These were women caught in a certain socio-economic situation—low housing areas, living and working together. The spectres of their lives were similar: having to find day-care, having to find certain kinds of situations. They arranged to share baby-sitting responsibilities, and it was working very well. There was no distinction of who was Black or White, who had what, who had a two-bedroom apartment or a three-bedroom apartment. There was no distinction. And then it so happened that one day they had some special guests, some special visitors, people from the ministry who for some reason were coming into the general area. And then it turned out, unplanned, that in the course of discussion, the Black women (myself included) found themselves responsible for the kitchen work while the other women saw themselves as those who would work the door, meet the guests, shake their hands and make the speeches. And we thought, there is something wrong here. The other women were saying that there was no thought as to who should do what, or to give jobs to people on the basis of skin colour or where they were from or what status they had. Why do I remember this incident?

The third story has to do with the National Black Coalition of Canada, a group that went through the whole struggle of putting together issues related to Blacks, whether American, Canadian, African or Caribbean, in Canada. The meetings were always hectic. One day, at a meeting chaired by one lone Canadian Caribbean Black woman, the men were raising one point of order after another with references to *Robert's Rules of Order*. It got so bad that she could not get that meeting contained. Frustrated, she stood up full height and said, I am a Black woman conducting a Black woman's meeting, and I do not want to hear about no dead Black man called Robert! Well, there was dead silence. Why do I remember this?

The fourth incident involved a meeting of the Congress of Black Women in Edmonton—fascinating discussion, interesting dialogue, looking at issues, looking at strategies, thinking about the things we could say to policymakers. We thought we really had everything said and documented. And there was one statement made by Glenda Simms, conference president, in the middle of a discussion of issues pertinent to beauty contests, something about Black women not being seen as sex symbols but as sex objects. This was a small point in the midst of a heavy discussion on strategy. The next day the headlines read, "Black Women Not Sex Symbols, They Are Sex Objects"—that was the extent of the paper's coverage of the entire conference. Why do I remember that?

Please keep those four stories in mind as I speak, to see if connections can be made to real issues. The first story involves someone who has gone into the Third World, done really good work, is really sensitized, and then walks up to two Black people and asks them, picking them out from all the others, if they know where he can find a domestic. The second story shows how one is shaped by one's past experiences—the group-of-women-with-child-care story. Some people do one thing and some people something else based on something that is there, not purposefully set out but, at the same time, which comes out. The third story shows that when we attempt to do something, we tend to bring to it a certain experience coming from a certain kind of situation. A Black woman could not lead a Black people's meeting without reference to rules put together by a White man. And lastly, the situation of a Black woman and sex symbols and sex objects as headlines.

As we pull together the strands, we are left to try to make our world a more decent, humane, humanitarian and pleasant place to live. Just in case you didn't know, that is the purpose of this conference. Never mind the big title, "Rethinking Development," because that is what we have been attempting to do, to make this world more human and the things we do more humane and decent for people in the world.

I think we must be conscious of some oversights and the concerns that have been expressed (and that I feel) about the failure of this conference to address and include the women's critique and viewpoint as an integral part of the discussion. Of all of the topics covered, the issues pertaining to women and development are not peripheral. They are not something to discuss after you've discussed all the other issues. Women constitute 50 percent of the world's population.

I am not an economist, I do not know anything about numbers, but the authorities say women put in 66 percent of the world's work-hours. They are the backbone of human settlements and a substantial part of the paid labour force. They are important decision-makers in areas such as family size, nutrition and health. It would be illogical to see women in development as an optional frill, as something to give token recognition to.

It is said that you shouldn't bite the hand that feeds you. I am very pleased to have been invited here, but I will not apologize for my critique. Many of you, sensitive to this information, will feel with me this feeling of frustration and disillusionment when men and women with the expertise you have, expertise in the area of human resources, expertise in politics, economics and development, come together and then we compartmentalize and put women's issues into one workshop which ran concurrently with other things we wanted input into.

Experience shows that issues pertaining to women are normally discussed in three stages. It is my feeling that we should have been at stage three, not stage one or two. In stage one, women feel the need to separate themselves, to find out where they are, to work out their platform together. In stage two, we know our situation and expect to be on every panel so we don't have a panel of people talking about issues that would not include the feminist or women's viewpoint. (I should not use the word *feminist* because it is like *sex* used to be before we could say *sex*—it has a certain connotation for some people. I am going to use *women* rather than *feminist* just in case you've got that block and everything else I will say will get blocked because the term *feminist* has implications for you.) In the third stage there is no need to talk about the issue because everyone is sensitive to it.

Models of development have been discussed, but any model which does not give primary importance to the needs of women and the promotion of human development is deficient. So those of you who are discussing models, those of you who have economic models, must look for ways in which the model you have will include the women's perspective and the promotion of human development. Any model would be deficient if this perspective were left out.

There are three approaches to women's issues (I stole this from Peggy Antrobus): the justice approach, the expediency approach, and the wisdom or feminist approach. I will put the few remarks I have left in the framework of the justice approach, from the vantage point of a Canadian citizen with roots and emotional ties and interests in the Caribbean. I strongly feel that I know both worlds and that I operate in both worlds on a daily basis with few contradictions. I could give examples, but I'm sure to an audience like you are, examples would be superfluous.

Who are we, Caribbean-born Canadian women? I will borrow words from a Philippine woman who spoke at an Ontario visible-minority women's conference: " In a predominantly White society, we are Black or Coloured; in a male-dominated society, we are subordinate; in a profit-oriented society, our labour is the cheapest; in government priorities, our needs are the last to be met if not the first to be ignored." I thought this was powerful and I couldn't say it better.

Often we are referred to as immigrant women—even when, in my case, we have been in this country since 1960. I am referred to as an immigrant woman despite the fact that I have my Canadian citizenship and feel that I am part and parcel of the whole Canadian milieu. I am always being asked the question, where are you from? There is always that reminder that you do not really belong or that the sense of belonging is not there. This overt and covert labelling and stereotyping has a negative impact on our integration into Canada's organizational structures. When I say organizational structures, I am talking about the structures to which many of you belong.

Caribbean-born Canadian women have solidarity with their homelands. We avidly read or listen to any reference to happenings there. We support our families there financially and otherwise. Some of us still own little bits of whatever is called property there, and we have all kinds of vested interests in our homelands. We visit often, and we nostalgically recommend our island to all Canadian friends. We feel ignored, we feel slighted, we feel disenfranchised when we are not sought out, consulted, informed or given the opportunity to comment where there are programs, projects and other ways in which we can have input into what is happening in Caribbean development, especially on issues pertaining to women.

I am not here to discredit those of you who work in this area, those of you who have access to information and agencies, but we often hear of certain Canadian women's exploits, returning from X project or program in Y island. We feel slighted as we sit through the presentations and are lectured on what is happening there. The assumption that we have no knowledge, reflections or expertise to offer, as we are given this analysis by the experts who have been there, demoralizes us.

There are ways in which we can create outreach from the organizations to which we belong. It could be just an information sheet saying the next project is taking place on this or that island. The complete lack of consideration as to what is happening to Canadian development programs in the Caribbean is distressing to us. We are caught in a double-jeopardy situation that surrounds us in this Canadian mosaic: sexism and racism. We have not really addressed the question of racism, but it is something we live with in this mosaic on a daily basis. The stereotyping that occurs gives rise to the assumption that we are no longer involved there or here. And so there is that world of no-women's-land. We are caught in a situation where we are neither ambassadors for Canada nor ambassadors for the Caribbean. It's going to be interesting to observe the contingent that goes to Nairobi to celebrate the end of the UN Decade for Women. Anybody taking bets on the colour of the faces that will be going?

We have to be placed in areas where we can be part of the selection process, the policymaking process. Because we don't have access and equal opportunity, we are denied the networking that occurs. Being part of a visible minority, the networking that occurs in White Canadian society cannot be used by us in the same way.

Women's role in our Canadian society, as elsewhere, is changing. Society today demands more of women than the fulfilment of traditional roles. If I were performing traditional roles, I would have a husband, sit at home, go to work and come back, cook the meals. Roles are changing far more than the fulfilment of traditional roles, far more than the fulfilment of strictly biological roles. Caribbean Canadian women have remained further behind in the progress that has been made, compared to mainstream women. I mentioned racism and sexism. Caribbean Canadian women have remained almost out of sight in the leadership of the women's movement of this country. I am on the Canadian Advisory Council on the Status of Women. With 30 women from across the country, I am the only Black woman there—there is also one native Indian. I am in my second year of the appointment and I find it very difficult when I look at the council's material and research over the last 10 years because there is very little mention of visible-minority or Black women's issues. You cannot discuss women and the economy if you do not talk about women caught in the service industry, the women in the lowest rungs. Who are the women caught in the lowest rungs? Every time this issue is raised, you are made to feel that you are just being disagreeable, bringing up issues that the system is just not ready to deal with. But we carry on.

A joint task force on immigrant women in 1979 in Ontario showed at least seven or eight different major areas of concern: exploitation in the workplace, poor working conditions, lack of training for the job market, lack of knowledge regarding rights, deprofessionalization, job ghettos, requirements for Canadian experience, unemployment and underemployment—and those of you in the trade union movement should address these issues. I don't know very much about trade unions, but I think that the whole business of seniority, the whole business of moving up as a result of having been there a number of years, works against the newcomer. The major area of concern for Caribbean women is the underutilization of work skills. Inability to rise through the system adds to frustration in the workplace. There are too few opportunities for advancement and there is too little respect for foreign qualifications. I remember when I came from Grenada, I had papers, a school certificate, but I had a devil of a time trying to get someone to tell me I had what in Ontario is Grade XIII. Oftentimes it is thought that the day you come into this country is the first day of your life, and so you come with almost nothing. No one counts the fact that you had already lived 20 or more years of your life. Trade union people: maybe we could talk about this later, this assumption that we have no leadership skills and no administrative abilities, that we cannot be expected to compete with others from the mainstream, and that we should find our place in society and be nice and quiet about it.

Foundations and others concerned with development must look to and seek the involvement of Caribbean Canadian women with relevant qualifications and experience. As we declare the end of the UN Decade for Women, whose goals are equality, development and peace, all Canadian women, regardless of origin, regardless of race, regardless of creed, must come together to work a social change for peace, for justice and for the development of all. The whole peace movement is said to be underrun by women, but only by White women—Black people, it would seem, are not interested in peace. One can argue that efforts have been made and in some cases there are some positive advances, I am sure there are.

I mentioned earlier that women must be included in all aspects of development: social, economic, political, cultural and religious. A year ago I read a document put out by the Development Assistance Committee, which adopted some guiding principles to aid agencies supporting the role of women in development, and I ask all of you interested in working in that area to read that document.

It is my hope that my remarks can be placed into the context of this conference. I know there are many of you sitting there who could have made this speech much better than I have, who have expertise in the area and vast experience in convincing Canadians that we have to do more in the area of development. We not only must do more, we must do it better. Doing it better means starting here, starting with us, starting with a change in our attitude, and with our inclusion of Caribbean Canadian women, who have to contend not with only sexism but racism.

I would like to end with a few lines from a poem by a Jamaican woman:

Now, against the bitterness of subway trains,
my heart beats songs.
Some wheels say freedom,
the others: home.
Still, if I can balance water on my head,
I can juggle worlds on my shoulders.

Workshop Sessions

THE ROLE OF THE STATE
IN DEVELOPMENT

Summary of Presentations

by Michael Kaufman

The four papers took not only different regional objects of analysis but different conceptual objects as well. Together they demonstrate the variety of current Marxist discussion on the state. As Chairperson Colin Leys noted at the end of this conference session on the state, after fifteen years of sometimes dry and torturous debate, the payoff is becoming evident.

The contribution of **James Petras** (Sociology, State University of New York, Binghamton) was an exercise in conceptualization of the state (the full text of Petras's paper can be found in a companion volume to this publication, *Rethinking Caribbean Development*). He touched on the contradictions between different parts of the state apparatus or, in his words, between the three distinct "states" that form the capitalist state. These contradictions—between the repressive state, the patronage state and the technocratic state—result from differences in their position within the overall state and from differences in the particular way that class struggle and the political, economic and social needs of the system affect them. Indeed, at one level we can read Petras's paper as a discourse on the importance of class conflict and struggle on the shape and operations of the state in particular capitalist societies.

Turning to the Caribbean, Petras polemicized against what he saw as neo-liberal visions of the state and against attempts to recreate an East Asian development model in the region.

The presentation by **Rick Williams** (Social Work, Dalhousie University, Halifax) was a good mix of theoretical discussion and concrete investigations of a particular region. He was interested not only in contradictions between different functions or structures of the state but in contradictions in the arena of policy.

He noted that in Canada's Atlantic Provinces there has been a relative overdevelopment in the welfare function and an underdevelopment of the state's capacity to aid the accumulation of capital. This disparity results from the impact of the class struggle and also from the requirements of legitimation. His discussion was an implicit challenge to strictly functionalist views of the state and also to a reductionist view that would see the state operating solely according to the logic of capital.

Peter Phillips (Government and Sociology, University of the West Indies, Mona, Jamaica) made a presentation on state-to-state relations and the overly murky topic of imperialism (the full text of Phillips' paper may be found in a companion volume to this publication, *Rethinking Caribbean Development*). Phillips provided a periodization of U.S. economic and political relations with the Caribbean in the twentieth century: the first period was one of U.S. expansionism from 1898 to the end of World War II; next was the consolidation of U.S. hegemony in the postwar years; and, finally, the late 1960s and early 1970s opened a new period, a period of challenge to a U.S.-controlled Caribbean. In providing this periodization, Phillips highlighted the need to understand the fluid character and specificity of imperialist relationships at any given time.

Gary Webster (Political Science, University of Prince Edward Island, Charlottetown) again showed the importance of concrete regional and local analyses of the state. His discussion of the impact of the state on economic development in the small province of Prince Edward Island showed some of the antagonisms at the level of the state, and between the state's patronage and legitimizing functions and its role in managing a capitalist economy.

Commentary by Michael Kaufman

(Michael Kaufman is with the Centre for Research on Latin America and the Caribbean at York University, Downsview, Ontario)

Each paper raises important questions and issues for research and analysis. After reading the paper by **James Petras**, I was left feeling a need for further theoretical discussion and concrete analysis of the specific articulations and contradictions within the three states, and in relation to the demands of capital.

Such analysis has an important bearing on our strategies of change, particularly for those of us living in bourgeois democratic countries where the state becomes one arena of struggle and contestation. The unsuccessful experiments in Chile and Jamaica, for example, showed the many stumbling points awaiting those who engage not only in struggle against the state but struggles within the state. This is not to suggest that a socialist strategy that starts with an election to governmental power is erroneous; it is to suggest that the struggle is only beginning at that point.

I would want to question some of Petras' assumptions about neo-liberal visions and "magic of the marketplace" ideologies in the Caribbean. I think he reads a bit too much into the U.S. experience on the one hand and into the current fascination of some Caribbean leaders with the Puerto Rico,

Singapore, Taiwan and South Korean models on the other. I agree with Petras's critique of these models and with their inapplicability to the Caribbean as a whole. However, in Jamaica, to cite the most apparent example, Seaga's free-enterprise and pro-USA stance is combined with a technocratic and statist view of Jamaican development. Local capital is up in arms against exchange controls, and it was Seaga, not Manley, who nationalized the Esso refinery that provides the island with its gasoline and oil products.

Rick Williams' discussion of the contradictions between the provision of welfare and social services and the more limited needs of the market economy raises interesting questions about the state and about our whole analysis of capitalism. Marxist thought has traditionally stressed an analysis of relations of production. It was not until the new wave of socialist feminism that we saw a rise of interest in an analysis of capitalism as including determinant relations of the reproduction of labour power. These relations vary over time and from society to society but have as a common feature the predominant role of women within an arrangement controlled by men. Intriguing questions exist as to whether these particular reproductive relations are intrinsic to capitalist production, whether they are even fully functional for capitalism, and how class struggle and sex struggle shape this realm. What is the role of the state in relation to the daily and generational reproduction of labour power and to the class, gender and authority systems instilled within the family? The whole realm of welfare and social services relates directly to these questions.

When I read **Peter Phillips'** contribution, I think of the need to continue to disaggregate changes in economic relations and state policy. For example, many changes in U.S. policy towards the Caribbean started in the middle of the Carter administration in the late 1970s. I do not think anyone would argue that there was any straightforward causality—the economy has been sliding for many years. Rather, ideological determinations and political expediency were key. Indeed, if we advance a few years to the introduction of the Caribbean Basin Initiative, we see a plan that is actually opposed by certain sections of U.S. capital. The periodization itself and the changes within the periods also show the impact of the international class struggle. In the case of changes in Carter's policy, the impacts of the struggles in Iran, Nicaragua, southern Africa and, to a lesser extent, Jamaica were key.

Gary Webster's piece challenges us to extend our understanding of the unique characteristics of small states. For example, in a small country or province there is perhaps a greater need for a capitalist to be responsive to public pressure, lobbying, neighbourhood discontent and so forth. At the same time there are more avenues for patronage, personal manipulation and co-option. Interesting questions would be raised if we were to compare the experience in P.E.I. with the experiences in Grenada, with its roughly equal population, during the New Jewel revolution.

As a group, the papers raise a number of broad issues and questions, some of which have been mentioned above:

1. There is a need to push hard in extending our understanding of the state as an arena of struggle and contestation, without falling into dead-end, strictly reformist approaches.
2. Despite the weakening of its hegemony, the USA still wields tremendous power to subvert or destroy attempts at socialist transformation. How do we take this into account when developing strategies of change? There must be no illusions that simply going more slowly or quietly will stave off U.S. opposition. Reasonableness has never seemed to impress U.S. policymakers. How can we avoid pointless and self-defeating confrontations? A key lies in the mobilization of the population.
3. The implicit or explicit assumption of all these papers is the state as a capitalist state. The transformation to new socio-economic and political orders requires changes in the basic nature and function of the state. This means new relations of political, economic and social power and, in particular, the development of new institutions and means for power to be exercised at the level of the neighbourhood, workplace and schools. Concrete investigations of the strengths and weaknesses of such attempts is an important dimension of future research. One key issue is the place of political pluralism. What are the possibilities for drawing on the best of representative democracy and the best of direct democracy in a way which would minimize the disadvantages of each? (On this, see for example the interesting thoughts of C.B. MacPherson in *The Life and Times of Liberal Democracy*; and of Nicos Poulantzas in "Towards a Democratic Socialism," *New Left Review* 109 [May/June 1978]: 75-87.)
4. Finally, we understood that states in capitalist societies are capitalist states. This is one of those cosy canons of Marxism that forms the backdrop to all the widely varied approaches to Marxist state theory. What we are only beginning to analyse and understand—thanks to the contribution of socialist feminists—is the extent to which the state also embodies and helps preserve male domination. In what sense can we speak of current states as patriarchal states? How does this description of nature or function of the state as a capitalist state contradict its imperatives vis-à-vis the maintenance of a gendered system of human relations?

That so many questions and thoughts come to mind from a reading of these four papers not only indicates how far we have come in our understanding of state structures but also reveals the richness of the vein of inquiry that lies waiting to be mined.

INDUSTRIALIZATION AS DEVELOPMENT: MEGAPROJECTS

Summary of Presentations

by Chairperson Michael Clow

In Atlantic Canada, the word *megaprojects* usually brings to mind huge energy projects, though the label is applicable to a much broader range of massive-scale development schemes. These projects are often either embraced uncritically as sources of economic salvation or dismissed as rip-offs. In this session, three social scientists—two from Atlantic Canada and one from the West Indies—together presented an initial attempt to go beyond these popular conceptions to examine the experience of the two regions with megaprojects and the development strategies that underlay them. **Ralph Henry** presented an overview of the state-owned complex at Point Leisas in Trinidad; **Jim Bickerton** examined the "megaprojects strategy" of the Canadian and Atlantic Canadian governments; and **Andrew Secord** used the state-owned nuclear power–generating station at Point Lepreau, New Brunswick, as a concrete case around which to propose an agenda for further research into megaprojects.

Ralph Henry (Economics, University of the West Indies, St. Augustine, Trinidad) examined the Point Leisas project in Trinidad as a classic case of a small country attempting to transform its economy with megaprojects. The Point Leisas complex was seen in the context of development policy failures of the past and the changed external factors which set the conditions for what appeared to be a logical new development strategy consistent with the domestic politics of Trinidad and Tobago in the 1970s. After specifying the failings of this megaprojects development strategy, Henry asked whether Trinidad and Tobago might not have been better advised to have used its foreign exchange in managing a different kind of development, one that would have had a greater spread effect and a longer-term and more positive impact on the economy and society.

Henry offered several statistics as a way of introducing Trinidad and Tobago: a population of 1.1 million; an area of 2,000 square miles; third-highest per capita income in the Americas; an open economy, with oil representing 94 percent of its exports in 1980; and a government that is not nationalistic in its economic policy.

Henry proceeded to survey his country's development strategies, starting with the "Puerto Rican" strategy of the 1950s, when tax holidays and other incentives were set up to induce foreign capital to invest in the country, with an emphasis on export markets. This strategy did not create significant long-term employment and foreign exchange. The companies left when the tax holidays expired, moving to countries where better government concessions could be found.

In the 1960s, the government modified its development strategy to one of import substitution. Tariff barriers were established and were designed to stimulate a local capitalist industrial sector initially protected by tariffs that might eventually expand to include an export orientation. However, by the early 1970s, import-substitution industrialization had failed to improve income distribution, employment creation and foreign reserves. This was combined with intense social and political discord, exceptionally high unemployment, shortages of government revenue, and balance-of-payments problems.

The 1974 increases in the international price of oil quickly changed the economic development picture from bust to bonanza with new government revenue and a foreign-exchange surplus. The government then developed a resource-based strategy of industrialization which would use the hydro-carbon revenue to convert and transform the economy. This strategy had three objectives: (1) to increase the value added to be derived from natural resources through forward linkages, (2) to diversify sources of foreign-exchange earnings and (3) to transfer technology to the country and to upgrade the technical expertise of the labour force. Whereas the state had previously provided incentives and infrastructure for investment, it was now going to take a more direct role.

The centrepiece of this strategy was the development at Point Leisas, an area on the south-central side of the island of Trinidad. Substantial oil and gas was to be pumped into the area as energy and feedstock for a huge petrochemical complex to produce methanol, urea, fertilizer and steel. From 1974 to 1983, this megaproject took TT$3 billion out of the TT$7 billion spent on development.

By the 1980s the picture had come full circle, with a lack of government revenue, balance-of-payments problems and high unemployment. The expected benefits of the Point Leisas project had not materialized, but it had contributed to new problems. There was some technological transfer but, without an institutional base, this was limited. In most cases, foreigners are still required to operate the individual plants. The impact on the labour market has been negative. There has been very little employment created downstream in spinoff industries. The iron and steel component suffered serious losses as a result of a combination of protectionist measures in the USA and domestic production problems. In addition, the Point Leisas construction project became the wage leader in the economy. The massive increase in demand for construction labour, coupled with cost-plus construction contracts, raised real wages throughout the economy. The longer-run impact was an erosion of the country's international competitiveness in many of its traditional lower-wage sectors. The project has not yielded compensating revenue to equal oil and gas revenue when that is gone. It has also contributed to high mass-consumption patterns, which have implications for long-term foreign-exchange problems.

The project had seriouly disruptive social impacts. The funds invested in Point Leisas took money away from badly needed housing in a country where 35 percent of the population lives in substandard housing. The division of wealth has widened. Social problems arose as one area of the country received huge government expenditures while other areas did not.

In conclusion, Henry suggested the need for a different development strategy, one that would avoid the disruptive social impacts of the Point Leisas development while using oil and foreign-exchange earnings to create more even and resilient long-term development.

Jim Bickerton (Political Science, St. Francis Xavier University, Antigonish, Nova Scotia) outlined the federal and provincial governments' rationales for supporting the resource-megaproject strategy of economic development. He noted that resource *megaprojects* are not new in Canada, even if the word is, and that lately these projects have been concentrated in the energy sector. Indeed, Canada is the only country that has declared a reliance on megaprojects as its economic strategy. This megaprojects strategy emerged from the "industrial strategy" debate of the late 1970s and early 1980s. During the late 1970s, Bickerton argued, a number of conditions demanded that the state intervene to direct the pattern of growth during the 1980s and 1990s:

1. a world oil crisis and a continued rise of energy prices, which caused
2. a federal-provincial crisis in Canada, especially between Ottawa and the main oil-producing province of Alberta, and
3. a growing crisis in Canadian manufacturing, that included a $150 billion negative balance of manufacturing trade. Deindustrialization threatened if the state took no action.

With the return to power of the Trudeau Liberals in 1980 after the Conservative interlude under Joe Clark, a debate raged within the federal government over the proper response. The first proposal from Herb Grey and the nationalist wing of the party was an interventionist strategy to regulate foreign-owned branch-plant manufacturing so as to enhance domestic benefits from the manufacturing sector, and to use the Foreign Investment Review Agency (FIRA) more aggressively to bring about a more productive and competitive manufacturing base in Canada. This strategy was opposed by an anti-interventionist group whose counterproposal was to rely on Canada's supposed "comparative advantage" in the resource-export sector as the basis of future economic growth and development.

Their argument was that the terms of trade between the 1980s and the year 2000 would favour resource exports as compared to manufacturing, and therefore Canada should further exploit her resources for export as the basis of her economy.

This second approach prevailed and was encapsulated in a 1981 policy statement entitled, *Economic Development for the 1980's*, which proceeded on three premises:

1. investment opportunities would be in resource development, not in manufacturing,
2. a potential of $440 billion in resource (oil, gas and nuclear) megaprojects existed, and Canadian manufacturing's niche was in supplying inputs to these projects and in developing the industrial expertise and capacity for expanding into world markets on this basis, and
3. the government could not control foreign investment, nor could it resist internal and American opposition to economic nationalism of the sort seen in the National Energy Program.

However, this national megaproject strategy met its demise as soon as it was declared, killed by changes in the world economic conditions upon which it was predicated. Most importantly, the price of oil fell and oil became a surplus commodity. Megaproject planning was based on a rise in the price of oil to $70 per barrel by 1990, and the collapse of oil prices and markets undermined both the strategy and the federal-provincial price agreements built around them.

In the Atlantic Provinces, however, the enthusiasm of provincial governments for megaprojects did not wane. Megaprojects appeared to be the instrument that would, once and for all, cure these provinces' economic woes and involve them, at last, in a major role in a national economic strategy. Provincial governments in New Brunswick, Nova Scotia and Newfoundland saw great potential for forward and backward linkages in manufacturing and began hyping local businesses to "gear up" for the "inevitable" boom and its industrial spinoffs.

Newfoundland's conflict with Quebec over Labrador hydro-power expanded into a battle with Ottawa over control of offshore oil and gas. Like that of the government of Nova Scotia, Newfoundland's official enthusiasm was based on the original megaproject strategy assumptions: high oil and gas prices and ready markets, terms of trade favourable to manufactured goods, and industrial spinoffs that could be captured by domestic manufacturers so something would be left once the boom in resources was over.

Related to these assumptions, Bickerton pointed out, are the perhaps fatal weaknesses of the megaprojects strategy:

1. unfavourable world market conditions,
2. falling energy prices,

3. fierce international competition,
4. extremely high capital-intensivity, with high capital-borrowing costs, and
5. no real optimism that local firms would in fact supply the major industrial inputs into megaprojects despite intense official hype.

Bickerton concluded that in spite of the problems that could be seen, the temptation of this strategy seemed to be too attractive for governments to resist. Hopes for regional prosperity based on the classic Canadian pattern of resource exports proved overwhelming for the impoverished Atlantic region, and Atlantic Canadians bought in on the schemes. Bickerton noted that there was not reason to believe the resource gamble would succeed in Atlantic Canada, because it had failed elsewhere.

Andrew Secord (Economics, Saint Mary's University, Halifax; and Saint Thomas University, Fredericton, New Brunswick) stressed the necessity of understanding megaprojects within the social and political context in which they arise. Such an approach to the Point Lepreau nuclear reactor megaproject in New Brunswick leads one to an analysis which goes beyond a description of the impact of the project to an explanation of why the project was undertaken. His paper proposed such a research agenda, derived in an elective fashion from a survey of the international political economy of development literature. He argues that only explanatory research is of use to communities that wish to understand the process of megaproject development so as to challenge or modify megaproject planning or create alternative development paths.

In 1973 the government of New Brunswick announced that the government-owned New Brunswick Electric Power Commission (NBEPC) would construct a 630 megawatt CANDU nuclear reactor at the tip of Point Lepreau on the Bay of Fundy in southern New Brunswick. The Lepreau project was to be state-owned and state-financed and to utilize the CANDU technology developed and sold by Atomic Energy of Canada Limited, a federal state agency. By completion in 1982, the Lepreau nuclear reactor had a capital cost of $1.4 billion, almost entirely debt-financed by the utility on foreign money markets. At that time, the Lepreau project debt load (guaranteed by the Province of New Brunswick) was greater than the accumulated provincial debt for all other purposes. The project was planned as a pre-build with one-third of the contract for export. At completion, slightly more than one-half of the power was designated for export to the United States. NBEPC is presently investigating the possibility of a second nuclear reactor at the site that could export 100 percent of its power output to the USA.

At the time the decision was made to construct the nuclear reactor, there had been very little publicity on the implications of the project. The New

Brunswick government's economic analysis was very limited. It reduced energy policy implications to the "standpoint of power economics," accepted NBEPC's assumptions concerning the demand and supply of power and carried out no analysis of the costs and benefits of the project relative to alternative investments. NBEPC was left to decide on the viability of the project based on its internal corporate criteria, and the provincial government saw its role as one of modifying the adverse allocational impacts of the project by, for example, minimizing unnecessary infrastructure costs and ensuring an adequate supply of labour for the construction phase. Members of the public who were opposed to the project argued that one could not assume that what was good for NBEPC was good for everyone in New Brunswick. Their critique focused on the questionable need for the project and on the project's adverse impact on electricity rates in the province. Their position was argued by the Maritime Energy Coalition before the Energy Committee of the New Brunswick Legislature in 1980. In that brief, they estimated that Point Lepreau nuclear energy would be twice as expensive as present system costs, and they argued that more efficient alternatives were available, the financial risk was too large given the size of NBEPC, and the alternatives would provide more employment. Both the government and the Maritime Energy Coalition took positions within a neoclassical economic framework.

Secord then surveyed the research agendas that are suggested by the international development literature, restricting his analysis to three perspectives: (1) the neoclassical, staples perspective, (2) the "development of underdevelopment" approach and (3) the Marxist dependency perspective. In each case, he brought out research questions relevant to the Point Lepreau megaproject.

1. The traditional evaluation of megaprojects attempts to quantify project costs and benefits within a *neoclassical economic perspective*. Although this evaluation might conclude that the Point Lepreau project was uneconomic and unnecessary and has serious health and safety risks, its framework would not provide an adequate explanation of why the project was undertaken or why another nuclear power plant is being planned and promoted by the provincial government.

2. In searching for an explanatory focus to the research agenda, Secord then looked at the "development of underdevelopment" perspective and Marxist dependency theory, both of which are distinguished from the neoclassical approach by their emphasis on power relations, class interests, and mechanisms of exploitation. The *development of underdevelopment perspective* (associated with A.G. Frank) emphasizes the mechanisms of underdevelopment, where development on the periphery (and the Maritimes would be placed here) is a reflection of development at the metropole. Mechanisms such as unequal exchange, and surplus appropriation by successive layers of elites culminating at the metropole, operate within

a worldwide capitalist system, which itself is the universal cause of under-development. The result on the periphery is blocked capitalist develop-ment, a drain of economic surplus, stifled industrialization and a distorted development process. From this perspective, a megaproject on the periph-ery is a reflection of development elsewhere. A series of questions then follow about the relationship of the state to capital elites, as the mechanisms of the expropriation/appropriation process under conditions of unequal exchange are identified and quantified.

3. The *Marxist dependency perspective* includes three different schools: the "associated dependent development" school (Cardoso, Faletto), the "modes of production" school (Laclau) and the classical Marxist approach (Kay, Warren). All three approaches have fundamental similarities that distinguish them from the neoclassical, staples perspective (Rostow, Schumpeter, Innis, early Watkins) and the "development of underdevelop-ment" perspective.

The *associated dependent development school* criticizes the "development of underdevelopment" perspective on the grounds that it suffers from the limitations of a formal mechanistic model. Instead, the "dependent devel-opment" school stresses the importance of analyzing particular concrete situations within a particular historical social process involving class con-flict and class formations. The "dependent development" approach in-cludes three components: the external (general determinants of the world capitalist system), the internal (specific structures and social organization), and the interaction of the two in particular concrete situations. This allows a dynamic analysis of how external and internal factors interact to condition the movement of societies. This leads to an analysis of structural linkages, coincidences of interests among classes, the impact of general trends on specific relations, and the dynamics which result. For the Point Lepreau nuclear reactor project, this approach suggests an examination of the class structure of New Brunswick, the history of class alignments, the relative power among factions of the capitalist class, specific corporate/govern-ment economic and institutional alignments, and connections among fac-tions of the capitalist class in New Brunswick, Canada and the world.

Modes of production writers emphasize the dynamic of capitalism and its ability to generate its own economic surplus. Surplus is understood not only as appropriated from but as generated in dependent peripheral societies that are structurally articulated with international capital. This approach suggests questions about the ways that surplus is generated; the locations of generated surplus; the role of the state in capital accumulation; the factions of the capitalist class among which surplus may be locally distributed; the relationship between surplus generation in the periphery and surplus transfer to class factions at various metropoles; and the histori-cal development of capitalism, in which class conflict may or may not be an important factor at any particular moment in history.

From the "modes of production" perspective, a nuclear reactor in the periphery is seen within the context of state activity to assist capital accumulation (on the assumption that a nuclear reactor has little coercive or legitimizing function). This approach suggests that little can be said of the particular project unless one has an understanding of the social formation of which the provincial state is a part. This raises several questions concerning: the nature of the capitalist class, capitalist class factions and their relative powers, the contradictions of the capitalist class at that moment, the degree of autonomy of the provincial state relative to capital, the identity of the contractors, direct and indirect benefits to various groups which might be grouped into class factions, the relationship of labour elites in the construction industry to conservative political interests, and the way in which a nuclear reactor reduces contradictions for the capitalist class in the periphery. As these questions indicate, the "modes of production" approach and the "dependent development" approach overlap considerably.

The "modes of production" approach has been criticized for its reductionistic and mechanistic materialism, and for overlooking the role of ideology, political action, collective consciousness, class action and human energy. These criticisms raise questions with respect to the Point Lepreau nuclear project about the importance of mass culture, the extent of local control of the cultural process, and the concentration and centralization of cultural institutions, all of which may explain the role of subjective (class or interest-group) consciousness on the outcome.

In conclusion, Secord sees his work as social research that proceeds from specific concrete situations and is part of a process of community reflection and action. Out of this process, communities, groups and individuals will understand whether megaprojects have anything to do with development as they define it.

Without being engaged in the process of defining development, social scientists are often left to accepting the state's range of categories of development or to imposing the categories and definitions of one theoretical framework onto the concrete situation. If these were the only two choices, social research could do little more for the people affected by the Point Lepreau nuclear reactor than identify them as either unknowing accomplices or unwilling victims of that megaproject.

Conclusions by Michael Clow and Andrew Secord

(Michael Clow is with the Department of Sociology, Saint Mary's University, Halifax, Nova Scotia)

Our knowledge of the concrete interests behind individual megaprojects and of the best theoretical framework within which to explain the appearance, enthusiasm for, and general failure of megaprojects as development schemes remains incomplete.

Although the word *megaprojects* is relatively new, the similar characteristics of most megaprojects, i.e., (1) the enormous scale, cost and capital-intensivity of the projects, (2) the central role of the state, and (3) the hopes for development from manufacturing inputs and downstream spinoffs, are not. These characteristics could be identified in Canada in a whole series of projects, e.g., the construction of the Canadian Pacific Railroad in the 1870s and 1880s, the hydro development of Niagara Falls in the early part of this century, and the creation of the St. Lawrence Seaway in the 1950s. Megaprojects are not a new category of economic project, though the numbers and capital-intensivity of these schemes are escalating rapidly, as is dependence on them. Our understanding of these trends has not really progressed beyond the level of analysis found in the tradition of Lovins' work in the "hard energy paths," which remains fundamentally within the liberal mode of explanations. How megaprojects are tied up with the structure of corporate capitalism and the development of the contemporary state is not well understood.

These presentations reinforce the notion that the state and state activities are crucial to the building of these projects (whether "successful" or "unsuccessful" as profitable enterprises). Forms of state action clearly range from incentives, subsidies, risk underwriting, and financing to indirect or direct ownership, but why the state is a necessary central actor in various projects warrants further investigation. Why megaprojects? Why a megaprojects strategy on the periphery of North American capitalism? The explanations are still at only a preliminary, largely descriptive stage.

The consensus of the papers was that megaproject strategies have been developmental failures and are likely to be also in the future. The implications of these failures for capitalist development on the periphery and at the centre is unclear. Do they represent a temporary pause on the path to greater capital-intensivity and scale of production caused by fluctuating world economic conditions in the current prolonged crisis, or do they signal the fundamental unviability of the "hard path" and a "business as usual" future for resource capitalism?

As noted by all participants, the need for an alternative strategy of development is pressing, very difficult to chart and difficult to imagine receiving support under existing political and economic conditions. The continuing support of the megaprojects strategy in the face of apparent general failure is only evidence that the megaprojects phenomena is in need of much deeper analysis.

MODELS OF
AGRICULTURAL DEVELOPMENT

Summary of Presentations

by Terrance White

The workshop on agriculture consisted of two presentations, one by **Argelia Tejada** (President, Research Institute for the Dominican Republic) and the other by **Anthony Winson** (Director, Gorsebrook Research Institute for Atlantic Canada Studies, Saint Mary's University). At the conclusion of their presentations, **J.T.G. Andrew** (Deputy Minister of Agriculture for New Brunswick), made some remarks concerning the presentations. The session was chaired by Bob Thompson.

Tejada and Winson gave interesting views of the present capitalist system and how its operation affects agriculture in the Dominican Republic and in Atlantic Canada respectively. Both presenters were aware of the obvious disadvantages that each suffered by being on the periphery of the system and of the relative ineffectiveness of government action in improving the situation under the current political and economic set-up. Andrew differed somewhat from this position but did confirm some of the points raised by Tejada and Winson.

Argelia Tejada (abstract of paper follows) felt that the role of agriculture in the capitalist development of the Dominican Republic was to increase production (including for export), to keep people in the country and to increase peasant income. In her country there have been attempts by the government to modernize, and to eliminate problems associated with the ownership of most of the agricultural land by only a few people. In the mid-1960s there was a reorganization of land tenure by which most of the large estates were expropriated. In the redistribution of land by the government, only males received land. This, she felt, was a source of continuing problems associated with agriculture in her country.

In the Dominican Republic, the present state agricultural objectives seem to be realistic but their effect has not always benefitted the people. Moreover, there is danger, Tejada said, in being tied to an international market.

The state would like to be self-sufficient in food, and farmers concentrate on rice production. They want to keep the cost of food low by producing it themselves rather than importing it. They want to increase their production of food for export and to raise the income of producers. However, crops produced for the world market have increased while crops produced for the internal market have decreased. Competition for land and resources favours the foreign market. Crops that were consumed locally (fruits and vegetables) are now exported because of their increased value. Fruit is being replaced in the national diet by bread and spaghetti. Food prices within the country are being driven up. The peasant farmer suffers because his production is not integrated into the national economy.

Considering the experience of the past twenty years in the Dominican Republic, Tejada made several points. In her opinion, state strategies in agriculture had not worked. She felt that a political decision would have to be made to change landholding practices and that women must be included. The increase in production for the export market has had bad results for most of the population—profits go to the few, and the many have less food.

Anthony Winson (abstract of paper follows) outlined the experience of Atlantic Canada from about 1850 to the present. Basically he argued that the fate of agriculture in that region was determined by the free-trade policies of the nineteenth century and the deindustrialization and the generalized crisis in other types of primary production of the early twentieth century.

Winson used Ontario as a point of comparison for the Atlantic region. He noted that both regions had similar early histories with developing agriculture and industry. The difference in the two regions (and the parting of the ways, so to speak) had to do with the relationship between agriculture and industry.

The wheat of Ontario stimulated the whole economy, raising farm incomes and providing the manufacturing centres with markets. This prosperity enabled industries to become established. Later, after the end of the wheat economy, farmers were able to go on to mixed farming because of the urban populations then present. The manufacturing sector was also able to continue to grow.

The Maritime situation developed differently for various reasons. One reason was the dominance of merchant capital. The merchant class protected its interests, which often discriminated against local agriculture and business. Also, the use of farm machinery by Maritime farmers was less than in Ontario by 1971.

The industrialization which occurred in the Maritimes is often said to have matched or surpassed that of Ontario in the 1880s and 1890s. A home market developed around the growing industrial centres and there was some transition to mixed farming.

Then the Maritimes were deindustrialized. By 1921 (and probably by 1910) the pattern for Maritime agriculture was set. Livestock production dropped, the farm population declined and there was a decrease in improved land.

After 1945, some of the small farms survived because of high prices resulting from wartime recovery but, when costs rose by the 1950s, many

Maritime farms had to increase in size or produce more, which many could not do. The farm labour force declined. The number of small and medium farms declined (85 percent disappeared between 1941 and 1981). There was a decline in improved acreage (50 percent between 1941 and 1981). There was a decapitalization of farming in Atlantic Canada but an increase in capitalization of farms in the rest of Canada. The output of Maritime farms stagnated after 1961, whereas Canada's output on the whole expanded.

Winson concluded by making the point that, when compared with Ontario, the Maritimes are underdeveloped. The regional phenomena has a direct relationship to the deindustrialization of the region but was not apparent until after World War II when the "tractorization" of agriculture began.

Commentary by J.T.G. Andrew

by Terrance White

J.T.G. Andrew was the discussant. He introduced his remarks by noting that for years he had been listening to people telling him "why we are where we are" but with little advice on how he was supposed to do what he does. His experience in agriculture goes back many years, and he has now reached a point where some analyses of agriculture take into account some of the things done years ago that were clearly wrong.

Andrew noted that he enjoyed listening to Argelia Tejada's discussion of what a logical and well-balanced strategy should be. Like all strategies, he said, when one actually tries to implement it, one finds that it has all kinds of unplanned side effects.

In reference to Anthony Winson's analysis of Maritime agricultural development, Andrew said the practical side of it boils down to: How does one make things actually happen when there isn't time to analyze all the inputs? Since 1972 he has been trying to make development take place in New Brunswick's agriculture within a regional and national economy. He would agree with Winson's comments that, in general, regional agriculture has been declining steadily since the Second World War, including in New Brunswick. The fundamental reason behind the decline in New Brunswick's agriculture in the 1950s was that people had come to believe that what they should have out of life, especially in material goods, was clearly not available in the context of New Brunswick's small-scale farming economy. For the producer the question was: Do I stay in at the survival level or do I try to participate in the "great new world of tomorrow" being portrayed by the mass media? The options paternalistically defined from the national level were essentially, if one wished to participate in this "good life," one had to pack one's bags and leave for other parts, whether it be Alberta or wherever.

In New Brunswick's case, Andrew maintained, the government has had some success by aiming at world markets with room for expansion (e.g., blueberries, hogs, apples and strawberries). It has been especially difficult to promote the livestock industry in the Maritime region, principally because of the absence of a local grain industry. Historically it has been cheaper to produce a hog in Alberta and ship it here than to produce it locally. Andrew attributed the failure to develop a wheat economy to the climate of the Maritimes.

The central government system in Canada, he noted, tends to maximize the general economic opportunities by putting all its investment into agriculture in Ontario because Ontario produces things more cheaply than the Maritimes. Agriculture Canada, like many other federal departments, concentrates on single sectors and does not think of the holistic environment in which agriculture operates in Atlantic Canada or of the wider social effects of taking away production here and transferring it to Upper Canada.

Andrew noted that Third World development aid was replete with problems as well. One of these has been the lack of individuals with the necessary experience to advise on agricultural development aid. Personnel in his department have been involved as implementing agents for the Canadian International Development Agency (CIDA) in agricultural development projects. Every time he gets involved in an aid program and goes to talk with his counterparts in the Third World, he finds they are fighting the same problems in the agricultural and marketing spheres as he is fighting in New Brunswick.

A Holstein cow, for example, to produce most efficiently, has got to have certain conditions surrounding it. Before agreeing to ship cows to Nicaragua, they went down, not to see what the political environment was like but what the physical environment for the cow was going to be. The problem is you cannot put a modern, efficient dairy cow into the hands of a poor small farmer and expect to get out of it enough to justify the initial investment in the animal. So, if you like, the change in technology in the animal that may be required may be totally counter to the dialectic of the environment in which you wish to put the beast. This problem is one that faces developing countries irrespective of the political climate of the country in which the cow is placed. When it comes to growing things, these common technical problems must be confronted if you wish to have the productivity and the progeny you are looking for.

It has been noted that about 12 percent of New Brunswick's agricultural production is related to one multinational enterprise. Andrew said, we do not worry too much about this, because in this case most of the benefits trickle down in the province, where the firm is based. If one studies the case history of the potato since 1910, we are growing approximately the same number as we were 70 years ago. The market we were shipping to up to 1950 has almost completely disappeared—the table-stock market in Montreal,

Ottawa, Toronto, etc. Now 50 percent of our potatoes go to Mr. McCain for processing into French fries, and he buys 60 percent of them by contract and the other 20-40 percent "on the street." If we didn't have McCain, we wouldn't have a potato industry, because the decline of the table-stock industry, with the growing self-sufficiency of Ontario and Quebec, and the development of cheaper and more efficient production techniques on P.E.I. were squeezing us out of the potato business.

It has never been possible to get potato farmers in Canada to give up playing poker every year and to develop an organized marketing system so, instead of being gouged by the middleman and the consumer, they could do a little honest gouging themselves. If you look at the price of potatoes over the last few years, making no allowance for inflation, the high and low prices were achieved in the 1950s, and there has been no real increase in return since then.

Discussion: There was not much time for discussion at the end of the session but the final comments by **Tejada** were, first, that supply and demand is bad for small farmers. Second, the state should "interfere" and guarantee the farmer a living. Third, the multinationals have more economic power than some countries and the "people" are in an unequal position when dealing with them. The system as it presently operates means virtual enslavement for millions of people and a loss of political power. The large companies have only profit as their motivation and are not concerned with the welfare of people.

Abstracts of Papers Presented

Argelia Tejada: *Development of Agriculture in the Dominican Republic*

(the full text of this paper can be found in a companion volume to these proceedings, *Rethinking Caribbean Development*)

Most efforts aimed at modernizing agriculture in Third World countries measure development by technological innovations in the work process and the increased production of agricultural goods. This vision of development obscures the fact that historically the cause for change in agriculture has not been technology. On the contrary, the transformation of agriculture in the capitalist developed societies of today was fostered by the urban industrial class. The reproduction of capitalism is determined by urban industry and to a much lesser degree by social relations inside the agriculture sector.

Henceforth, development strategists must take into consideration the contradictory relationship of agriculture and industry to explain the causes of agricultural backwardness in Third World countries and to find global solutions. If development plans for agriculture do not consider the whole of society and the role played by its economy in the international division of labour, the secondary effects of isolated technical innovations can have negative impacts on the whole economy.

I will summarize some conclusions about the capitalist development of agriculture in the Dominican Republic which are derived from the empirical research I have done in this area. Capitalist development assigns agriculture certain functions to generate a self-sustained process of industrialization. Synthesizing, the main functions of agriculture in Dominican society are:

1. to fulfill the internal demand for raw materials and food by increasing the production and productivity of the peasant sector,
2. to increase non-traditional agricultural commodities for export,
3. to retain the labour force in the countryside to diminish job pressure in the cities,
4. to offer a cheap labour force to agro-industrial capital,
5. to increase peasant's income, which would tend to expand the internal market for the consumption of industrial goods, and
6. to transfer value from the agricultural to the industrial sector.

Agriculture effectively fulfils only the role of offering cheap labour to industrial and agrarian capital. Other functions are insufficiently performed, which creates obstacles for the socio-economic development of the whole society.

State policies and activities to raise agricultural production have been ambiguous, reflecting the class contradictions inside the state itself. The most radical state policies in agriculture were concerned with changing land tenure. In general, large landholdings belong to absentee owners who in many cases engage themselves in other professional or economic activities. As a consequence, landowners do not constitute an isolated class whose main source of income originates in rent or direct exploitation of the land. Rather, cattle raising has become a peripheral activity for merchants, bankers, industrialists and liberal professional people. In too many cases, the holding of a few cows is an excuse to preserve large holdings of non-cultivated land by warding off state appropriation or peasant invasion.

This situation explains why the industrial sector firmly opposed the execution of the agrarian reform laws, even though agrarian reform is an important tool in capitalist development. The political agreement which took place in the Dominican Republic in 1965 joined transnational and national industrial capital with the commercial sectors and latifundista holders. Fear of communism makes the industrial class nervous about policies which question private ownership of land. This was especially true after the popular uprising of 1965 which ended with United States Marines invading the country for the second time in its history.

Conclusions

1. State agricultural strategies aimed at promoting self-sufficiency, increasing income for peasants, earning more foreign exchange through agricultural exports, and keeping down the cost of food have not met the expectations of improved living standards in the rural areas. The small size and dispersion of peasant farms works against efforts aimed at increasing their production and productivity. Capitalization takes place in large and medium farms oriented towards exportation, but the dominance of large landholdings dedicated to cattle raising keeps major extensions of land unproductive while aggravating the problem of unemployment in the rural area. State goals cannot be met without a political decision to change the structure of land tenure in the country. This decision has been rejected by interests with greater control of the state apparatus. Peasants' struggles for land have been militarily suppressed. Since the promulgation of the agrarian reform laws, little has been done to put them into practice. State loans and technological assistance to farmers are no substitute for the needed transformation of the land-tenure structure.

2. International conditions in the last two decades have accelerated profit-making in agriculture for exportation. Transformation of traditional peasant production into the production of agricultural commodities for export, often under foreign ownership by multinational corporations, has created a need to import food to meet the basic needs of the population. This transnationalization of agriculture implies not only a vulnerability to the fluctuations of commodities in the international market and the devaluation of local currency but a change in traditional eating habits. Populations already malnourished must suffer greater deprivation to feed populations already enjoying abundant food, among whom dieting has become an obsession. Production does not necessarily benefit the producers. On the contrary, corporate control of agriculture or individual control of large landholdings means that increased production goes towards huge profits for the few but provides less and poorer food for the many. We might end up with modern monopoly capitalism and, at the same time, widespread poverty and dependence.

3. Agricultural development must be an integral process in which farmers themselves own, care for and use the land. Agricultural production must be oriented towards meeting basic needs and creating the basis for the industrial process of the whole society.

Anthony Winson: *The Uneven Development of Canadian Agriculture: Farming in the Maritimes and Ontario*

(a version of this paper can be found in a companion volume to these proceedings, *Rethinking Atlantic Canadian Development*)

Leading authorities on Canadian agriculture (Mitchel 1975, Hedley 1978) have argued that agriculture must be considered an underdeveloped sector of the Canadian economy. Typically this is justified by reference to high rates of exit from this sector, the low return on capital investment, historically lower wages, declining production in certain sectors and so on.

However, I contend that a historical and comparative examination of the question reveals that in the Canadian context, the underdevelopment of agriculture is more usefully viewed as a regional, rather than a national, phenomenon. A comparative examination of the rural development of the Maritime Provinces and Ontario supports this argument.

The Early Role of Merchant Capital
This section notes the early importance of the wheat economy in Upper Canada in providing farmers with sufficient disposable income, and farm families with the commodities they needed. Later, when Upper Canadian farmers lost their preferential position in the British market and wheat went into decline, the existence of a viable industrial sector eased the transition to a system of mixed farming in that region.

In the Maritimes, the absence of an important wheat economy meant that a home market for industry was given less impetus. Nevertheless, a market was potentially provided by the development of a vigorous shipbuilding industry and by the square timber trade.

However, merchant dominance in the Maritime colonies meant the continuation of a free-trade policy favouring the import of cheap foreign manufactured goods and American foodstuffs. As Acheson (1972) notes, this policy delayed the development of local industry and agriculture by at least two decades.

Industrialization and the Home Market
The period after 1870 saw the rapid growth of manufacturing, including heavy industry, in the Maritimes. This created a substantial increase in the urban population as the labour force engaged in manufacturing expanded. This development provided Maritime farmers, for a time at least, with several home markets for their produce, including Sydney, New Glasgow and Trenton, Saint John, and Yarmouth. The strength of these markets was crucial for the successful transition from farming practices based on field crops to mixed farming, where livestock comes to form the main component of a modern agriculture.

Deindustrialization and Its Impact

Recent economic historiography has shown that after 1900, with a series of crises of overproduction and with the centralization of the Canadian banking system, much of Maritime manufacturing was either absorbed into Central Canadian concerns or driven out of business. Alexander (1977) notes that between 1880 and 1890 the gross value of manufactured goods per capita in the Maritimes grew from 63 percent to 68 percent of that of the rest of Canada, but by 1937 it had fallen to only 42 percent of Canada's. In the 1920s, Maritime manufacturing had grown at a rate of 0.7 percent, as opposed to 6.1 percent in Central Canada.

The deindustrialization of the Maritimes naturally had a direct impact on the manufacturing labour force, and hence on the size of the home market for Maritime farmers. Employment in manufacturing began to shrink after 1891 in New Brunswick and Nova Scotia, when it had been on a par with that of Ontario. By the late 1930s, the proportion of the population engaged in manufacturing in Ontario was three times that of the Maritimes.

This industrial crisis in Atlantic Canada was coincident with price depressions in the forestry and fishing industries as well. Given the partial dependence of many farmers on these activities, Maritime agriculture was especially hard hit by economic circumstances in the pre–World War II period. Evidence of this is to be found in census data showing the low level of capitalization of Maritime farms relative to Ontario, and the relatively low proportion of "improved acreage" on farms.

The Third Technological Revolution and Maritime Farming

The Second World War and the labour shortages it occasioned impelled the beginning of the third technological revolution in Canadian agriculture— the introduction of a mobile source of power on the farm as embodied in the tractor. This new technology had a bias towards large farms, or those with the ability to expand the land base of their operations.

Although farm commodity prices were kept stable by federal government policy, prices for farm inputs produced by an increasingly monopolized agribusiness sector were not. The result was an increasingly serious cost-price squeeze for Canadian farmers after the war. This, in turn, created more pressure to utilize costly machinery and other inputs. Farms in the Maritimes were smaller to begin with and generally capital poor. They were thus not in a good position to adapt to the exigencies of the new economic climate.

Agribusiness and Regional Agrarian Decline

Another key factor in the post–World War II rural environment was agribusiness. In the Maritimes particularly, an asymmetrical relationship between the rapidly dwindling number of farmers on the one hand and horizontally and vertically integrated agribusiness enterprises on the other has characterized agriculture in the region. In New Brunswick and Nova Scotia, one or two firms constitute the dominant or only market for most of the farm produce in important sectors such as potatoes. Such firms are also the purveyors of all manner of agricultural inputs. As one study dealing with the situation in New Brunswick put it:

> Potatoes are grown on McCain land (Valley Farms Ltd.) enriched by McCain fertilizer (McCain Fertilizers Ltd.), using McCain seed (Foreston Seed Co. Ltd.). Harvesting is done with McCain machinery (Thomas Equipment Ltd.) and the harvested potatoes are either stored in McCain facilities (Carleton Cold Storage Co. Ltd.), sent to McCain's plant for processing (McCain Foods Ltd.), or sold fresh. In the latter case, the potatoes are handled by McCain shippers (McCain Produce Co. Ltd.) which use McCain trucks (Day and Ross Ltd.) to move them to point of shipping. The processed potatoes can similarly be moved in McCain trucks (M. & D. Transfer Ltd.) for shipment abroad, where one of McCain's sales distribution systems (McCain International Ltd.) handles the marketing. (Senopi Consultants Ltd., "A Report on the Situation of New Brunswick Potato Farmers for the National Farmers Union," 1980, p. 24-25.)

Regional agribusiness has used strategies of importing potatoes and then re-exporting them to their U.S. operations, and of controlling substantial amounts of prime agricultural land to gain control of the potato market and secure cheap supplies for their operations. However, there does not seem to be evidence of a unilinear trend towards the takeover of farming by agribusiness firms as some have suggested. It would appear to be more a case of processors reducing their dependence on "independent" farmers for supply as much as possible and thereby bolstering their leverage in determining the price for farm produce.

These integrated agribusiness concerns today face an ever smaller number of farmers with operations that historically have been small and undercapitalized. Moreover, these farmers have often been divided along generational, ethnic and ideological lines, as well as on the basis of their own economic circumstances.

The Failure of Maritime Agriculture
Apologists of the present system of agriculture have typically argued that the expulsion of the rural population from the countryside, though unfortunate, is in the long run desirable because it allows a consolidation of farms, a greater and more efficient use of farm machinery and a more efficient use of labour. Ultimately, the social consequences are alleged to be justifiable, given the substantial gains that can be made in productivity and in farm output.

Although this rosy scenario may have some relevance to the experience of agriculture in Ontario since the 1940s, it is called into question by the Maritime experience. The consequences of the postwar process of rationalization have been significantly different in the two regions. To begin with, the decline in farm labour in Maritime agriculture was three times that of Ontario in the intercensal period of 1951-61. Improved farm acreage is another indicator of regional divergence. In this regard, Ontario, despite a much higher level of postwar urbanization in its prime farming regions, witnessed a decline in improved acreage of only 19 percent from 1941 to 1981. In Nova Scotia and New Brunswick, improved farm acreage fell by approximately 50 percent during the same period while, in Canada as a whole, improved acreage increased by 18 percent.

Perhaps the most telling indicator of agricultural change is the fluctuation in the number of farms. Again, an interregional comparison is interesting. Ontario saw a decline in total farms of about 54 percent between 1941 and 1981 while, in New Brunswick and Nova Scotia, the total number of farms declined by approximately 85 percent. Only in P.E.I. did a gain occur in any size–category of farms—the very largest farms.

Two other indicators of regional agrarian decline are worthy of note. One is the decapitalization of Maritime farms that has occurred in recent decades. Indeed, data for 1961-71 show a decline of approximately 7 percent in the total value of capital (measured in constant dollars). For Canada, the value of agricultural capital had risen 23 percent during these years. Another indicator is overall output. Gross output stagnated in the Maritimes during the thirteen-year period after 1961. At the national level, output increased at an average rate of 50 percent.

This interregional comparison of some key data on Canadian agriculture suggests that we are not speaking simply of the restructuring of agriculture in accordance with the needs of Canadian capitalism in its advanced state, but rather of the failure of a regional agriculture.

Conclusion

In Canada the success or failure of regional agricultures in recent times was largely determined in the nineteenth and early twentieth centuries.

Ontario developed a vigorous wheat economy by the middle of the nineteenth century that provided a home market for a strong and diversified industrial development. This industrial structure was maintained and even expanded into the twentieth century, and it provided a vital local market for Ontario farmers once their export trade in wheat dried up. In Ontario, commodity production in agriculture became generalized in the last century as farm size expanded and capitalization advanced.

In the Maritimes, however, the continued predominance of merchant capitalists supporting free-trade policies throughout most of the nineteenth century, together with the deindustrialization of Maritime manufacturing and the generalized crisis of other types of primary production in the early years of the present century, seriously undermined the development of rural commodity production.

The absence of a dynamic expansion in farm size and an inability to capitalize their holdings in the decades up to 1950 spelled doom for the majority of Maritime farmers in the post–World War II period. It was in this epoch that the pressures of rapid technological change in agriculture and of integrated agribusiness operations with considerable economic power forced producers to reorganize their holdings and/or engage extensively in wage labour to remain on the land.

In Canada the underdevelopment of agriculture should be seen as fundamentally a regional phenomenon, historically related to the state of local industrial and commercial development. My interpretation therefore takes issue with the contention of those such as Mitchel (1975, Chapter 1) who say that underdevelopment is a condition that has characterized the whole of Canadian agriculture in recent years.

MODELS OF FISHERIES DEVELOPMENT

Summary of Presentations

by Chairperson Gene Barrett

The importance of the fishery for world development has progressed so much that observers now speak of the "blue revolution." The experiences of fishery development in the West and the Third World are converging as large-scale Western technology is diffused abroad, as Third World countries adopt Western management schemes for husbanding their resources and as similar organizational problems emerge in both plants.

The exclusive preserve of economists 20 years ago, fishery social science has now emerged as a leading area of interdisciplinary research and development planning. This workshop brought together planners, government officials and university-based sociologists with a wide variety of backgrounds and experiences to discuss complex issues of fisheries development. The presentations illuminated three leading issues in fisheries development.

The first issue is the relationship between the resource and development. Since fish stocks are a renewable resource, the primary biological problem has been to assess the potential volume of fish that is exploitable (the so-called total allowable catch) without threatening the resource base. The development problem for nation-states is to determine to what extent this total catch is being utilized within its coastal management zone. It is not an oversimplification to say that Third World fisheries havé generally been underutilized while fish stocks in developed countries have been overexploited (and, as stocks in the West have been depleted, or as fishery fleets have been restricted in their exploitation of these fisheries, the Western fleets have moved into Third World areas—this is particularly the case for shrimp).

The primary planning issues for the Third World at the harvesting stage of fishery development have been to increase the commercial catch and to increase its consumption to alleviate nutritional deficiencies. The papers by **Lennox Hinds** (Canadian International Development Agency) and **Svein Jentoft** (Institute of Fisheries, University of Tromso, Norway) both posed this problem at the outset. The artisanal fishery becomes the main focus of projects that stress the importance of mechanization and improved techniques to increase productivity. The Hinds paper carefully drew attention to the many considerations and lessons that have emerged from these efforts within the Caribbean context. In Western countries the issues relate more to conservation, with a focus on regulation to save fish stocks from overexploitation. As **Peter Sinclair** (Sociology, Memorial University, St. John's, Newfoundland) pointed out (abstract of paper follows), the many twists and turns of government policy in Canada and the latest agonies of the Kirby Commission all stem from this concern.

The second issue that social scientists have been concerned with in the fishery is the nature of income and the distribution of rewards. The impetus for this in the Third World stems from the absolute levels of poverty and unemployment that exist in rural maritime areas. In the West these problems are less acute and the main thrust comes from a concern with equity or lack thereof.

Improvements in productivity in the artisanal fishery and increases in the numbers of commercial fisherman are seen as important mechanisms for combatting poverty in the Third World. As Hinds points out, planners have to be cognizant of the relative returns offered by marginal investments in equipment and the real possibilities that debts can quickly overshadow incomes. This problem has always plagued Western fishermen. The technological imperative, fueled by relative prosperity (albeit often in the illusory form of credit) and competitive pressures to catch more fish, has led to a credit-debt trap that threatens to consume most Western fishing enterprises. Regulatory schemes originally designed to preserve fish now attempt to preserve fishermen.

This political-economic reality underlines much of what is new in the Kirby Report. Enterprise allocations, catch quotas, gear licenses, and seasonal regulations that vary according to geographical (ultimately socioeconomic) criteria have been designed in an attempt to impose some form of income and catch equality on fishermen. As Sinclair shows, these recommendations of the Kirby Report still fail to consider a number of more imaginative solutions that would be community-based in nature.

Of late, social scientists have become particularly concerned with the relationship between income and efficiency. Large-scale economies in the harvesting sector have become dubious in the long run because of the environmental damage wreaked by dragging technology. At the same time, intermediate-scale economies are being seen to underlie the nature of "appropriate" technology. This is the substance of the success stories in the artisanal fishery, according to Hinds.

The third issue in the fishery is the nexus of all successful fishery development projects, organization. Jentoft's paper concentrates on the central problem in the industry, its intersectoral basis. Fish is an extremely delicate and perishable product that needs individualized attention and immediate processing if it is to be consumable. The perishability problem plagues all stages of the fishing process and is exaggerated by intersectoral bottlenecks in transportation, communication and marketing. Also, fish reproduction and habitation is largely outside of human control. Hence fish catches are a gift of nature and are often unpredictable from season to season (or even trip to trip). Gluts and scarcities of fish landings are a hallmark of the industry, and they plague and stymie the best efforts at co-ordination. The organizational forms that have emerged in the fishing industry to cope with these problems range from very resilient decentralized systems, where each function is largely autonomous, to highly centralized, state-run corporations. The paper of **Orestes Gonzales Caballero** (Ministry of Fisheries, Cuba) provides an overview of one such state system in Cuba.

One of the most interesting issues to emerge in studies of the fishing industry in the last decade has been a discussion of the relative advantages and disadvantages associated with private ownership in the industry. Some view the instabilities in the fishing industry as being aggravated by capitalist enterprise, which puts a premium on competition, short-term profit, technological expansion, and centralization. The "normal" contradictions that plague capitalist enterprise at large are seen to be that much worse in the fragile and unstable environment of the fishery. Large-scale, state-owned enterprise is an interesting alternative to this model since it is not subject to the same competitive pressures or, in theory, the same need for short-term profitability. (Much more work has to be done on the effects of large-scale organization in the industry, however.)

Co-operatives are often seen as a viable alternative to both the small-scale middleman and capitalist models. Jentoft's paper explores the checkered career of the co-operative movement in the fishery. Co-ops have become of particular interest in the Third World, where savings are minimal and grass-roots organizational forms are needed to tackle the multifaceted needs of the industry while also addressing the social needs of the community. His study of a case in Nicaragua was particularly insightful in this regard.

Abstract of Paper Presented

Peter Sinclair: *Another Lost Chance? The Fisheries, the Kirby Report and Newfoundland's Underdevelopment*

(the full text of this paper can be found in a companion volume to these proceedings, *Rethinking Atlantic Canadian Development*)

The Kirby Task Force Report and its recommendations seem to indicate the loss of another chance to seriously address and redress the overall problem of Newfoundland's underdevelopment. The Kirby Report perpetuates an interpretation of Newfoundland's economic development which has ignored the potential of the fisheries to generate wealth and employment in a more diversified, albeit fisheries-based, economy. Consistent with public policy over the last century, there remains a lack of vision and a lack of commitment to a regional economy based on its major renewable resource.

Concerning itself with the creation of economically viable, large, centralized fisheries enterprises, its recommendations ignored both the central role of the state in allocating income and "success," and the basic conflict of interest between catchers and processors over the price of fish. Focusing on the health of large, centralized, preferably privately owned enterprises, it produced a document that was acceptable as a basis for policy formulation to the federal government, the Conservative government of Newfoundland, and the major capitalists in the fishing industry. The interests of fishermen and regional development were accorded second place. Where state regulation is recommended, it is done so reluctantly, as a last resort. More radical changes in the social organization of the region are simply not discussed.

The big processors of fish, the least economic of all parts of the processing sector, not the fisherman, were to be assisted by the injection of new capital from the government in the form of direct grants or loans. Further centralization of capital, accompanied by vertical integration from processing back to harvesting in an attempt to reduce uncertainty over the control of fish supplies, is recommended, in the face of what Barrett and Davis ("Floundering in Troubled Waters...," *Journal of Canadian Studies* 19, no. 1, 1984) argue is the relative success of smaller, more flexible companies. Although the task force did not openly advocate the elimination of fishermen to secure stocks for the fleets of large processors, its recommendation of the elimination of price and income supports (vessel subsidies and capital assistance, unemployment insurance) would make it impossible for the existing num-ber of Newfoundland fishermen to earn adequate incomes from fishing.

Although the exploitation of Newfoundland's forests, minerals and offshore oil fits quite well into a model of dependency upon foreign capital as the origin of the province's underdevelopment, external domination has not been the primary reason for Newfoundland's weak fishing industry. In at least two periods, internal class and political factors have aborted the opportunity to move to more diversified development.

Between 1880 and 1920, the Newfoundland fisheries were mired in old and declining patterns of exploiting the fish resource, while the island's main competitors improved the quality of their products, adopted new technologies and threatened to push Newfoundland out of its principal market. Following World War II, another opportunity was lost. Although deep-sea harvesting and frozen fish production were now emphasized, no effort was made to build a capital goods sector in the fishing economy, and overfishing by foreign nations was permitted.

The crisis of the early 1980s presented an opportunity again, because the major actors were so weakened, and the problems of the fisheries so publically displayed, that radical alternatives might have been considered. Perhaps not surprisingly, the Kirby Task Force did not consider these alternatives but instead presented a "solution" for big capital in the fishery. Ownership of the fisheries by fishermen or communities was not even mentioned. That poor incomes in the fish-harvesting sector are the result of low fish prices and the lack of fishermen's bargaining power was skated over completely.

The alternative for fishermen is some form of collective ownership, such as regional or community producers, co-operatives in which both fishermen and processing workers could become shareholders. The acceptance of collective bargaining with short-term price subsidies, coupled with a long-term co-operative development plan, would have been a strategy that more honestly and squarely faced the social problems of the Newfoundland fisheries.

But more is needed: a vision of the fisheries as the motor of regional development. A policy to rationalize the fisheries by reducing labour input or by centralizing production should only be contemplated in conjunction with a plan for regional economic diversification.

Exactly what should be involved in such a plan is difficult to specify. Anticipated revenue from offshore oil might be wisely invested in the long-term future of Newfoundland. One obvious starting point should be the promotion of backward linkages in the fisheries. Is it really too late to join our North Atlantic competitors in a sophisticated, multidimensional fishing industry? Unfortunately, the restricted and conservative vision of the Kirby Report and the widespread approval of its philosophy in business and government circles are indicative that the latest opportunity to grasp control of the destiny of Newfoundland may have been missed yet again.

WOMEN AND DEVELOPMENT

Summary of Presentations

by Chairperson Mary Turner

This workshop's call for a new definition of development is the major original idea to develop from this conference. It is unfortunate that not all the people involved in the conference were able to hear the resolution that emerged, and even more unfortunate that many who heard failed to listen.

Peggy Antrobus (tutor co-ordinator of the Women and Development Unit, University of the West Indies, Cave Hill, Barbados; the full text of her speech can be found in a companion volume to this publication, *Rethinking Caribbean Development*) was the first speaker. Stating that the first issue confronting women was the question of power, her speech centred on the need to overcome patriarchal society. Both First and Third World women find themselves in a position of "structural powerlessness" that can be fought by recognizing that patriarchy is the common enemy and feminism the basis for women's solidarity.

There have been a number of programs stimulated in the Caribbean since 1975—the Year of the Woman—including the Caribbean Woman's Bureau of 1975 in Jamaica of which she has been a part. Antrobus noted a change in opinion since that time—a general questioning of the concept of development and the recognition of the need for a feminist analysis.

Antrobus stated that the wide gap between rhetoric and reality was the root cause of underdevelopment. Acknowledging the difficulties of dealing with new theories, she claimed that in both capitalist and socialist works there was no room for women. Because of the patriarchal nature of society, there has been no analysis of development from women's point of view. She stressed a need for the feminist viewpoint to be interwoven with development theory. Thus a new definition of development would emerge, with women an integral part—not merely attached to it or ignored altogether. She argued that women have to begin to assert their views on global political questions, from military budgets to Zionism, and not to allow themselves to be corralled into "women's issues." Third World women have already taken the lead in this and she urged others to follow. It is imperative that women build self-confidence outside the domestic realm.

Anne Bishop (Canadian University Service Overseas, union and co-op organizer in Pictou County, Nova Scotia) spoke next and referred to her work with rural Nova Scotian women. She established four different groups of rural women: those from away who had deliberately chosen their lifestyle; those married to farmers and fishermen, who had some form of independence; those from towns and villages who had contacts with others and independence; and the wives of inshore fishermen. She characterized women in this last group as functionally illiterate, with an elementary education, many periodically employed in the fishing industry. They had never made independent decisions, having moved from their parent's home to their husband's at approximately fifteen years of age.

Worker co-operative organizations were set up. The main objective was to help these women make independent decisions in life and to mobilize them politically. Issues tackled included literacy, day-care, women's health issues, management, and development, all in the hope that there would be progress towards political activity. As a result of this program, a new class of women had evolved, from one with few or no options to one with improved education, job security and a sense of their own power.

Bishop concluded that future services like this should concentrate on the economic arena and improve precapitalist skills such as farming. An emphasis on violence, shelter, health care and child care was also recommended. All of these would promote consciousness raising and political mobilization.

Jean Stubbs (labour historian, Havana, currently engaged in research on rural women in post-revolutionary Cuba; the full text of her paper can be found in a companion volume to this publication, *Rethinking Caribbean Development*) took up both themes of the previous speakers, pointing out that patriarchy is clearly recognized as a problem in Cuba, but the socialist system promotes a systematic political attack on the problem, which is largely left to grass-roots organizations, such as co-ops, to combat here.

Although the patriarchal system is present in nearly all societies, Stubbs noted that the very decision to break with the traditional notion of development in the capitalist world contributed to the growing challenge of the patriarchal system in Cuba. Grenada was the only recent example of an Anglophone island that had tried to break free from the capitalist development model.

Cuba has risen to prominence within the nonaligned movement and the international community at large precisely because it has achieved growth rates that cannot be defined—upgrading of rural and low-income groups, with health and education indices that parallel a developed rather than an underdeveloped country and make for a far more equitable social fabric. There has been a raising of women's consciousness, an attempt to address inequality and an attempt to incorporate more women into public life. The number of women in agriculture increased following the agrarian reform movement of 1961-63, with most women working on home farms while the labour force of the state farms was predominantly male.

Cuban women challenged these work-force percentages, feeling they were not high enough. The Federation of Cuban Women, although criticized by outside feminists, addressed women's issues at the power-structure level across all strata of society. The Family Code of 1975 discussed questions of family relationships, household sharing, reproduction, and sexuality.

Taking up the theme of Bishop's talk, Stubbs referred to co-op structures set up in areas committed to breaking down gender roles. So far it appears that women are more favourable than men to co-ops. These co-ops have allowed a decrease in the workload, and economic independence from salaries.

This new consciousness developed mainly among younger women, those in the middle age group being concerned with their families, and the older women being unable to change.

Lynette Mensah (Dalhousie University School of Nursing, Halifax) was the last speaker. Focusing on the conflict between patriarchal medical priorities and the needs of Third World women, Mensah spoke of the increasing number of women and families in developed capitalist societies without adequate food, shelter, and health care. Proper health care for all has been a long time in coming, and it appears a more creative approach is necessary. In developing countries, health care is mainly for those who are sick, with a meagre amount of attention being paid to preventive medicine or psychological problems. There is little attention paid to women, even though it is they who bear the responsibility for health care. In developing countries, where poverty is a cause of health problems, family planning is a key issue but contraceptive information is not freely available. Another issue is health care associated with pregnancy. Early, regular, high-quality care and nutrition counselling is needed to combat the high number of maternal deaths. A third concern is the high number of deaths from reproductive cancers.

Mensah made several suggestions for improving health care, among them using women's groups, improving community resources, and training health professionals to deal with the specific needs of developing areas rather than attempting to develop a health care system that simply replicates the Western model. Unfortunately, because of time limitations, **Mensah** was unable to finish.

Bishop and **Mensah** spoke on a practical level; their talks were most informative and gave the viewpoints of professionals working directly with people. However, **Antrobus** and **Stubbs** gave presentations that were more central to the issues of development, and some of their ideas were the groundwork for the further discussions summarized in the following report.

Workshop Report

by Michael Smith

The opening plenary sessions were characterized by the omission of significant critiques from the women's viewpoints and experiences. These critiques are important for a number of reasons.

First, conventional development theories equate development with economic growth and, for women, this economic-centred approach has reduced or given only slow-growing access to resources and jobs. It has forced trade-offs between employment and working conditions, and it has increased work burdens in subsistence activities and reproductive tasks. A people-centred approach to development is necessary if women are to be acknowledged as truly integral to the development process. Second, conventional theory pays scant attention to linkages between women's productive and reproductive work. Third, it gives insufficient recognition to gender-based hierarchies in the family, community, and society at large.

Conference plenaries did attempt to introduce a more people-centred approach but nonetheless neglected the vital new analytical tool the women's viewpoint provides. Moreover, while the Women and Development panel made an original and positive contribution to the process of rethinking development in the 1980s, the segregation of women into this workshop deprived other workshops of the women's constructive contributions.

We can only hope, for example, that the workshop on Models of Agricultural Development addressed the implications of women's multiple roles in agricultural production and that the panel on Race and Class, Labour and Migration and the panel on Employment and Unemployment considered the bases on which statistics on what is considered work, and especially women's work, are collected and analysed. Did the workshop on The Role of the State in Development come to grips with the positive contribution made by Cuba's socialist government, including, as one of our panelists established, efforts to challenge patriarchy?

Development perspectives in the 1980s must be informed by the substantial body of women's research, analysis and action if they are to have a significant impact for change.

On Sunday the final session on Women and Development was held. The large attendance, both male and female, showed that many conference delegates were becoming aware of the new directions being taken. This discussion, chaired by Jean Augustine, focused on two areas: (1) practical issues such as women's participation and child care and (2) patriarchal societies and the need for a new model of development, one of "human development." The basic ideas that emerged were:

1. A new development model must include women as an integral part of its framework.
2. The concept of development needs to be disaggregated from the concept of material wealth, that of underdevelopment from poverty. Human issues must be considered.
3. There are strengths and weaknesses in both developed and underdeveloped countries. These strengths must be promoted and utilized. Countries must not be judged by external value systems.
4. If the concept of development were to be redefined, there would be no need for the feminist argument. Such issues would be resolved automatically.

The ideas that grew out of all the meetings and workshops were expressed in a resolution read to the conference delegates at the close of the conference (see Concluding Sessions).

RACE AND CLASS, LABOUR AND MIGRATION

Abstracts of Papers Presented

Dorothy Moore: *Race and Class, Labour and Migration in the Maritime Provinces*

(Dorothy Moore is with the Maritime School of Social Work, Dalhousie University, Halifax)

This paper presents a perspective on the association between ethnicity, gender and class in the Maritime Provinces as a basis for discussion in the workshop on Race and Class, Labour and Migration. It places the discussion of work and the employment of people divided by class, gender and ethnic cleavages into the context of Henry Veltmeyer's discussion ("The Capitalist Underdevelopment of Atlantic Canada," 1979) of the Maritimes as an underdeveloped region within Canada that provides a reserve army of labour for the Canadian economy. Within the Maritime region—which still suffers from the after-effects of deindustrialization in the early part of this century and from continuing relative economic stagnation, high unemployment, and generally lower living standards than the national average—ethnic discrimination and gender relations have created an internal differentiation of job opportunity and living standards.

Class and Ethnicity
There are three important subordinate ethnic minorities within a population comprised mainly of persons descended from immigrants from the British Isles—Acadians (descendants of seventeenth-century French settlers), Blacks, and Micmac (and Malecite) Indians (descendants of the Amerindian population).

The class structure that emerged in the region has been associated historically with ethnicity through conquest and colonialism. Merchants, business owners, and government officials have been predominantly British in background. For a time, the self-employed and self-sufficient independent commodity producers could be viewed as a middle class, although in this century, with the capitalization of farming, fishing and forestry, their way of life has become unviable. This group largely consisted of those of British origin. There was a large, landless labouring class in which the oppressed ethnic minorities of Acadians and Blacks were overrepresented, but from which Micmacs were largely excluded. Differences have been reinforced by the concentration of minority communities in less advantageous locations. The patterns of discrimination and oppression set in motion by colonial powers became institutionalized in a de facto ethnic segregation which survived well into the twentieth century and is still evident today.

Occupations
Acadians have migrated to urban centres in large numbers during this century as employment in the fishing industry has contracted. Many have been assimilated into the majority, English-speaking cultures. Some 22,000 Acadians live invisibly within the Halifax-Dartmouth area today for instance. Visible minorities—the Blacks and Indians—have not had this assimilation route open to them and possessed even fewer community resources than the Acadians with which to survive. Blacks moved to urban areas in large numbers in search of jobs but, with some exceptions, have remained employed in the lowliest service occupations such as domestic work, janitoring, and road repair, if indeed they have had any job at all. Most Native people remain outside the regional labour force altogether. Many of the jobs they do have are in Native organizations and services on the reserves, which offer no other means of livelihood, being too poorly endowed to support any independent way of life.

Employment
Disparities of income and employment exist among ethnic groups in the region. Acadians in southwest Nova Scotia, the area with the most prosperous Acadian communities, have unemployment rates that are twice as high as those of majority-group residents, in spite of heavy out-migration. Black unemployment rates in Halifax are 30 percent and, in rural areas, as high as

80 percent. Unemployment rates among native peoples have long remained at disastrously high levels, as high as 90 percent and more. There is no reason to believe that disparities between minority groups and the rest of the population have been reduced, even though basic living standards have been raised over recent decades by social welfare measures.

Gender and Employment
Another aspect of differentiation in the region's labour forces is the nature of work for women of all ethnic groups. Women are mainly employed in the service sector or in support services in large businesses and institutions, and their employment is frequently non-unionized, low-wage, casual or seasonal. They constitute approximately one-third of the labour force but, in addition, many women have a second, unpaid job at home in caring for their families. Women from minority ethnic groups tend to be employed in similar jobs, but Black women, for instance, are predominantly in the poorest jobs, and especially in domestic work. One study of the disadvantages of Black women in the labour force noted that they are affected by racism *and* sexism, both of which subject them to exploitation. It noted that a higher proportion of Black women work outside the home, and that more of them are also heads of households.

Conclusions
Sexism and racism have had roles to play in the competition for scarce jobs and are likely to be sharpened in situations where heavy unemployment and a large reserve labour pool exist. Split labour market theory shows how discrimination on the bias of sex and ethnicity provides a means for manipulation of the economy, which can help to increase its stability. Discrimination can also divide groups of workers and weaken protests about working conditions and unemployment, thus reinforcing a sense of class differentiation among the work force. We must, therefore, conclude that ethnicity, class and gender are inextricably connected and utilized in the dynamics of capitalist structures. In an underdeveloped region such as the Maritimes, disadvantages of ethnicity and gender are especially entrenched in a large reserve labour pool.

Gail R. Pool: *Migration, Development and the Grenada Revolution, 1979-1983*

(Gail R. Pool is with the Anthropology Department, University of New Brunswick, Fredericton)

Introduction
The People's Revolutionary Government of Maurice Bishop faced three fundamental development issues: (1) food and nutritional improvement, (2) tourist development and (3) social and cultural mobilization. As a result of policies aimed at restructuring the Grenadian economy, many people left Grenada in the first three years, but by 1982 there were more arrivals than departures. By 1983 the majority of the people were behind the revolutionary policies, but there were important differences according to geographic area, economic sector, sex and age. With the U.S. invasion of Grenada in October 1983, there was again an overall outflow of Grenadians who no longer felt there was a future for them on the island.

Research and Conclusions
In 1982 and 1983, my wife and I carried out field and survey research in Grenada for one year. The survey was conducted between May and June in nine separate communities in Grenada and four in Carriacou.

Altogether 501 people were interviewed after the questionnaire was tested. The sample is representative by sex, age and parish. Aspects of social and economic life were covered under the following: (1) community attitudes, (2) land, (3) employment and education, (4) mobility and migration and (5) household information. This is a wealth of data which is only beginning to be analyzed, but a few results may already shed light on the role of migrants in the revolution, and the effect of the revolution on migration.

According to the survey results, there are an estimated 371,000 Grenadians living abroad, or about four times the population of the island. This estimate is based on a listing of the relatives Grenadians knew were overseas, and so may be underestimated. About 75 percent of the Grenadians living overseas were divided roughly equally among Trinidad, England and the United States, with about 9 percent in Canada and 12 percent elsewhere. Many who live on the island plan to go overseas although they would prefer to live in Grenada. Of those who plan to migrate, fully 44 percent would rather live in Grenada, which points out how much immigration is viewed as a necessary but temporary event.

It is clear from the survey that the majority of Grenadians in Grenada supported the revolution. When asked directly, 63.3 percent thought things in Grenada had improved, as opposed to remaining the same or getting worse. Only 17.6 percent thought things in Grenada had gotten worse.

As is usually the case in migration, sex and age have an effect on plans to leave, based on the possibilities potential migrants see for themselves if they stay or migrate. Older people do not plan to leave unless it is to visit their children or to return to the place they lived while overseas. Women tend to want to leave at earlier ages. In summary, migration from Grenada is affected by the usual social and economic factors, but it is clear that the revolution did not fundamentally change characteristics of potential migrants. We know that changed attitudes to community and society may have precipitated considerable out-migration as occurred in the first two years of the revolution. What this survey gauged was the substantial in-migration and the potential migrants after the revolutionary government had had a chance to prove itself. The attitudes to the changes were quite positive, and those who could benefit from the revolution were the least likely to plan on leaving, wishing instead to make their contribution in Grenada.

We returned to Grenada in 1984 and found a fundamental change in attitudes among the youth in particular. Some had turned to crime, others languished in the streets, and still others had left the island. There were two basic reactions to the demise of the revolution and the U.S. invasion. Many felt betrayed by the New Jewel Movement and did not want to have anything to do with the party or its survivors. This may even have been expressed by a dismissal of politics altogether. Others did not participate politically and were waiting to see if Gairy's party returned to power—only then would they decide what to do: migrate, lie low or support the Maurice Bishop Political Movement. However, many who had supported Bishop and the revolution saw little future in Grenada. There was a lack of vitality in all sectors of the population. Many had taken on some of the outward features of Rastafarian ideology and culture. Ganga consumption had become frequent.

Nearly all the revolutionary programs have been scrapped, but what cannot be eliminated is the knowledge Grenadian youths obtained during the revolution. Grenadians were proud of their country and saw a future for their island and themselves. Without these qualities it is difficult to see any solution to the problems of the Caribbean and Third World countries.

It is our responsibility to understand how revolutions develop and what programs and policies might be appropriate to small states and, most of all, to influence world opinion against travesties like that which befell Grenada.

COMMUNITY DEVELOPMENT
AND REVITALIZATION

Abstracts of Papers Presented

Tim O'Neill: *Community Development Policy in Canada*

(Tim O'Neill is with the Economics Department, Saint Mary's University, Halifax; the full text of this paper may be found in a companion volume to this publication, *Rethinking Atlantic Canadian Development*)

This paper provides an overview of the approaches used by the federal, provincial and municipal levels of government in Canada and by private co-operative ventures to promote economic growth and development and to maintain economic vitality in local and regional communities. Including an examination of the federal role, the discussion focuses on public and private sector activity in Nova Scotia.

Two "sizes" of communities are discussed: (1) communities in the "small sense," i.e., geographical areas smaller than a province, and (2) communities in the "large sense," i.e., geographic areas from provinces to the entire country. Federal policy has focused more on communities in the large sense than on the areas we more commonly refer to as "communities": municipalities and small groupings of municipalities. The term *local communities* is used to refer to the first type and *regional communities* to the second. The primary concern is with policy initiatives with respect to local communities.

Federal and provincial government programs for economic development and for maintenance of economic viability and vitality have largely focused on economic sectors and on regional communities (provinces and supraprovincial regions). All of these programs have affected local communities. The same can be said for any economic policy. What distinguishes local community–oriented programs is that such communities are the specific focus of development/maintenance efforts—designated local areas are the targets of a policy and not merely incidental recipients of its impact. Of course, a sectoral, general regional policy may, in actual application, be deliberately focused on specific communities. However, those communities will be chosen only if the objectives of the program can be met by applying the program in that particular location. Sectoral or regional goals take priority over the economic viability and vitality of selected communities.

At the federal level, the major exceptions to this pattern since the early 1960s include: (1) the Area Development Act's concentration on local areas suffering chronic and high unemployment rates, (2) the Special Areas Program, which specified local economies with a high growth potential, (3) certain subsidiary agreements under the federal-provincial General Development Agreements, (4) the short-lived and functionally weak Ministry of State for Urban Affairs, (5) the small-scale transfer of federal government offices from Ottawa to other Canadian communities, and (6) the experimental Community Employment Strategy program. The Cape Breton Development Corporation also represents an attempt to deal with the severe economic difficulties of a local community. This approach has not been applied to areas with similar problems in other parts of the country. The new (IRDP) program, with its tier categorization of communities to differentiate eligibility for location incentives assistance, represents a somewhat greater local community orientation than was the case during most of the 1970s.

The provincial governments of Canada have varied in their relative emphases on sectoral versus geographical development efforts. The poorer provinces, such as those in the Atlantic region, have tended to be more concerned about general economic development and sectoral (mainly manufacturing) growth than about specific communities. The creation of new employment and income has been more important than where it is located. Our research showed that specific local communities in Nova Scotia have received attention from the provincial government. Two growth centres or "winners" (Halifax-Dartmouth and the Strait of Canso area) have been the subject of subsidiary agreements negotiated with the federal government as well as of provincially financed programs, agencies and crown corporations.

Local areas have been very limited in the extent and type of community development activity they can engage in. The appointment of industrial commissioners to carry out promotional efforts has been the main activity of municipal governments in this regard. The emergence of private community development corporations to foster new economic activity and provide business and social services provides a new and flexible approach for communities and community groups to use to maintain and enhance their vitality.

A.A. MacDonald: *Community Development and Alternative Participatory Strategies of Development*

(A.A. MacDonald is the director of the Coady International Institute, St. Francis Xavier University, Antigonish, Nova Scotia)

This paper provides a critical assessment of the community development strategy and identifies alternative, people-based participatory development strategies.

Conceptual Dimensions of Integral Development

At its most general level, underdevelopment is usually defined by disparities among nations in control over natural resources and economic activities, access to commodity markets, availability of investment capital and the sharing of industrial technology (B. Hettne, *Current Issues in Development Theory*, 1978). The current debt crisis of Third World countries is a significant indicator of this type of underdevelopment. At the national level, underdevelopment is usually defined by disparities in access to economic opportunities and institutional amenities. Rural-urban differences in economic, health and educational benefits are taken as indicators of underdevelopment. At the local or regional level, underdevelopment is usually defined by subminimal levels of productive capacity and basic-needs satisfaction.

Unfortunately, definitions of underdevelopment tend to reflect ideological or theoretical orientations that focus only on selected conceptual dimensions of societal reality. The agent of social change, however, must deal with societal reality in all its complexity as an integral phenomenon. This holds true at all levels.

If the unit of orientation is the underdeveloped *group* instead of the underdeveloped geographic community or area, underdevelopment can be defined by:

1. personal deficiencies of the group members, such as lack of knowledge, volitional capability, occupational skills, self-confidence, personal identity and physical welfare,
2. collective or group deficiencies, such as lack of leadership, solidarity, organizational effectiveness and power,
3. structural deficiencies in the institutional systems of society which discriminate against the group in the allocation of opportunities and benefits, and
4. cultural deficiencies of the larger society in beliefs, values and norms which legitimize or permit human and institutional retardation in society.

(A fifth dimension could be added: ecological deficiencies, the unavailability or deterioration of natural resources; however, to the extent that existing resources are amenable to development, this dimension may be included under the structural or institutional rubric.) This definition of underdevelopment assumes that any people-based development strategy must liberate the underdeveloped group from a multidimensional form of disadvantage. It implies that development for the group must be an integral phenomenon that includes the growth of personal and group capabilities as well as the transformation of structural and cultural systems that regulate the allocation of societal opportunities and benefits.

Assessment of the Community Development Strategy
This paper is concerned with the local or regional level of development. According to the 1971 UN annual report, *community development* connotes: "the processes by which the efforts of the people themselves are united with those of governmental authorities to improve the economic, social and cultural conditions of communities, to integrate these communities into the life of the nation and to enable them to contribute fully to national progress."

This strategy, which enjoyed prominence in the 1950s and early 1960s, assumed that the following actions were necessary for development:

1. making the community or village the unit of orientation,
2. relying on existing community leadership and institutions for analysis and planning,
3. accepting "felt needs" as the basis for community action,
4. pursuing community consensus as a prerequisite for action,
5. accepting community homogeneity without attention to class, caste or ethnic differences, and
6. insisting on the necessity of voluntary input by the people, usually in labour.

However, the community development strategy generally failed to cope with the following obstacles:

1. the rigidity of local community institutions limited the community problems that could be undertaken,
2. the law and order approach of most Third World governments precluded attempts at reform of institutions,
3. definition of felt needs tended to reflect the needs of the more articulate and powerful interests in the community,
4. village development tended to be pursued independently, outside of national or regional development programs,
5. the organic concept of community ruled out dissensus or conflict,
6. local orientation did not take account of stagnation resulting from government paternalism and bureaucracy,
7. programs tended to be oriented to amelioration rather than reform, and
8. there was a tendency to be preoccupied with process rather than economic outcomes (UN, *Popular Participation in Development*, 1971).

These deficiencies of the community development strategy have given rise to a disillusionment with it as an effective method of social change. Nevertheless, according to S.K. Kinduka, it did call into question the strictly sectoral approach to development of the 1950s ("Community Development," in *Community Organization Practice*, 1975). Building human capacity and self-reliance among the disadvantaged through informal education and participatory planning remains a valid dimension of the development process.

Alternative, Participatory Development Strategies
Admitting the deficiencies of the community development strategy, there is still a need for a decentralized approach to development. According to the 1978 annual report of the World Bank: "Among the most difficult aspects (of rural development projects) is the establishment of systems within which the small farmers can themselves have a say in how programs are designed and implemented, and how their skills, expert knowledge of the local farming environment and their capacity to help themselves can be fully integrated into an overall effort."

The main reason for the failure of decentralized local organization may be its inability to guarantee an equitable distribution of opportunities and benefits among the participants in development. According to L. Ralston et al., "regardless of the form selected, decentralization in systems with weakly organized local units usually leads to further penetration by central power . . . decentralization usually favours the central government or the local elite" (*Voluntary Efforts in Decentralized Management*, 1983). Consequently, there has been continual effort to modify and develop people-based development strategies:

1. *Co-operative enterprises* may be a first alternative to the community development strategy. The principal criticism of co-operatives is that they have failed to respond to the needs of the more disadvantaged in society. According to A. Laidlaw (*Cooperatives and the Poor*, 1977), their ineffectiveness in the rural sector primarily has been the result of the arrogation of benefits by the co-operatives' more powerful members and the domination of paternalistic government bureaucracies.

In response to this failure, two approaches are being adopted: organization of informal pre-co-operatives, and modification of the structure of conventional co-operatives.

The pre-co-operative is a non-registered co-operative organization which avoids the legal requirements of the government's regulatory system. By remaining relatively small in size, it seeks to avoid the structural differentiation that inhibits direct member participation in decision-making. In India, Bangladesh, Nepal and Malaysia, co-operative organizers are turning their efforts to the organization of homogeneous socio-economic groups as pre-co-operatives (E. Amit, ed., "Organizing the Disadvantaged for Economic Power," 1981).

Structural modification of conventional co-operatives involves the adoption of by-laws which, among other things, require the composition of management boards and committees to reflect the class composition of the membership. This is being adopted in the credit-union system of South Korea and in the agricultural co-operatives of India and Nepal. Such by-laws have enabled organizers to obtain legal judgments which have forced elections to be held despite opposition from vested interests and collaborating public officials.

2. *Use of the legal or judicial system in favour of the disadvantaged* constitutes a second people-based development strategy, especially in countries that enjoy the rule of law. According to Kinduka, "Major structural reforms have rarely been instituted with the enthusiastic consent of those who are most likely to lose as a result of those reforms; a certain modicum of legal coercion is a necessary component of any effective strategy of social change." The success of North American Indians in their land-claim settlements illustrates this approach. In India and other developing countries, this strategy is being effectively employed by Christian Church–based and Gandhian-type organizations to enable tribal and landless tenants to realize their rights to land and public-policy benefits. Another manifestation of this approach is the establishment of informal community courts to settle disputes among conflicting parties.

3. A third strategy is *"situational" modification of behaviours and attitudes.* According to Kinduka, "if attitudinal and value modification do not necessarily precede behavioural or structural change, they may often follow them." This strategy was used by the Nova Scotia Department of Agriculture to change the behaviour and attitudes of Nova Scotia dairy farmers during the 1950s. Adoption of farm sanitary practices and attitudes was achieved through the licensing of milk producers, which required farm inspection by the Nova Scotia Department of Health. Licensing, previously rejected by the farmers, was accepted voluntarily in 1956 as part of a legislative package that included protection against arbitrary termination of milk contracts by distributors. This third strategy requires that the people in question place a strong value on remaining in the situation, subject to modification, and that they feel free to leave it even if at some cost.

4. A fourth people-based approach is *advocacy*, which involves non-violent confrontation and non-co-operation to pressure change in the behaviour or practices of established power systems. The organizing of "action groups" consisting of core elements of the disadvantaged has become a popular alternative to village organization in India and other Asian countries. The Chipco Movement in northern India has mobilized tribal women for the protection of their forest resources against the exploitation of commercial timber barons. In southern India, action groups are networking for greater power and impact.

5. *Conscientization* is a people-based strategy closely associated with the action group approach of Asia and the "Communidad de base" approach of Latin America. This strategy adopts a target group approach and emphasizes consciousness-raising among the disadvantaged. In contrast with the community development approach, attention is usually centred on the structural and cultural sources of disadvantage. Group action is combined with reflection to develop social change capacity among the disadvantaged. Popular theatre and other culturally based techniques are used to raise the consciousness of the disadvantaged.

6. *Political mobilization of the disadvantaged* is a sixth strategy for change. Although not commonly used, it has been employed effectively in India to obtain representation for the disadvantaged in local government institutions such as the Panchayat Raj. Generally it involves mobilizing a target group in support of its chosen candidate.

7. The *"project" strategy* of social change means taking a more integrated approach to development by placing emphasis on accessing public programs. Whereas non-governmental organizations previously tended to organize agricultural and amenities projects independently of or in parallel with government programs, disadvantaged groups are now being organized to demand and obtain their fair share of production inputs such as credit, agricultural technology and health services. Thus they are being integrated into the institutional fabric of their societies.

8. *Target-group organization* is an eighth participatory strategy. Associations of landless workers, women's health groups, small farmers' marketing schemes and slum dwellers' organizations are illustrations of this strategy. The organization of the Woodlot Owners' Association in Nova Scotia during the 1970s provides a concrete case for analysis of objectives, organizational methods and outcomes.

These eight alternative strategies do not include all of the innovative, people-based strategies of development but are indicative of the awareness that development strategies must achieve personal and organizational growth among the disadvantaged along with the transformation of the structural and cultural systems that regulate the allocation of opportunities and benefits within their societies.

FINANCE AND AID IN DEVELOPMENT

Summary of Presentations

by Hugh Mellon

Cheddi Jagan (Leader of the Opposition, Guyana) presented a paper entitled "The Role of the State in Development," written while he was flying back from a conference in Greece (the full text of this paper may be found in a companion volume to this publication, *Rethinking Caribbean Development*). The initial part of the paper outlined the nature of the state. Jagan described the state as "an instrument of a class or group of classes and social strata." Until 1917 there was only one kind of state: capitalist. In 1917 there arose a workers' state. Describing states as capitalist or socialist is a more accurate and scientific manner of outlining the options. Capitalism is based upon free enterprise, and socialism relies upon central planning.

Jagan emphasized that the Third World is not homogeneous in relation to these options. Some Third World countries have a capitalist orientation, thereby choosing to have policies antagonistic to their own workers. These policies reveal the strains of fascist dictatorships.

Some countries such as Cuba and Nicaragua have socialist orientations, and a number of Arab states have feudal characteristics. Aside from the use of the oil weapon, there is no Arab unity. Most Third World states reside within the capitalist framework.

Development is more than an economic matter for Jagan. There are interrelationships among the various spheres of human activity. Reference was made to the recent history of Guyana. Through imperialist opposition to nationalism, the CIA made Guyana the first victim of the Cold War in 1953. As a result, new economic policies and a new political party were put in place. This set in motion the following tragic chain of events: chronic budget deficits coupled with a government imposed from without led to government unpopularity, which led to state violence, leading to governmental electoral fraud and cruelty, leading to further state violence, producing ongoing repression. The International Monetary Fund (IMF) imposed sanctions, and economic decline continued.

Keynes, Jagan said, had produced a temporary solution. Inflation and unemployment are now too deep and strong to be dealt with in that manner. Developed capitalist countries are exporting their problems to the Third World. Meanwhile, the nations of the Third World are having problems selling their products.

We must look at the classes that have power in the Third World. People have long looked to the middle class for leaders. Even the workers have done this. Imperialist states use race to divert attention while they remain capitalist and comfortable.

Most Caribbean leaders are from the middle class. They have been educated in elite schools. This, Jagan suggested, has produced problems. A parasite elite has developed in the Third World. After prolonged capitalism, nationalization merely allows the petty-bourgeois class to rise socially. This helps to produce discontent and revolution.

Jagan made reference to the Santa Fe Doctrine as a guide to the thought of President Reagan. This policy statement followed the lines of the Monroe Doctrine and of the Truman Doctrine, which sought to isolate the USSR and Cuba. Use of the Organization of American States (OAS) in the Malvinas War may have weakened this link in Jagan's view.

According to Jagan, the solution to the development problem is not to be found in the Puerto Rican or Alliance for Progress models. Revolutionary socialist democratic plans are the way to go. Within the Third World there are four classes: petty bourgeoisie, intelligensia, working class and peasantry. Capitalism allows the petty bourgeoisie to become the bourgeoisie. The International Monetary Fund (IMF) fosters this by its capitalist conceptions.

If the working class and the peasantry are able to assume power, changes can result. However, Jagan stressed caution in analyzing such developments. The New Jewel Movement in Grenada was the left wing of the petty-bourgeois class. Under Castro, Cuba has become communist. Progress can only be fostered through a move to communism; otherwise capitalism reappears. For example, since there is only a small working class in the Caribbean, the petty bourgeoisie is a stronger group.

Jagan closed by referring to his family's background as plantation workers and to his American education, which, he believes, has given him a more democratic viewpoint.

Jagan was asked how he would change things if given the opportunity. In reply, he stressed the need to educate people on the nature of imperialism and to move with them to workers' control. He argued that Forbes Burnham had played the fascist card in Guyana and had bribed his supporters to keep power. Ideological discourse is needed to break down the fears of the various ethnic groups. Jagan pointed to growing unity within the Guyanese labour force. Discrimination and corruption must be overcome. This seems to be happening within Guyana, as official government candidates for union office have been defeated. Technical assistance and especially education were seen as helpful where they did not involve tied aid and/or bilateral contractual restraints.

Jagan was questioned as to what role he saw for co-operatives. He responded with references to Robert Owen and Engels. Although co-operatives are good in and of themselves, they are only able to function for the benefit of the workers within communism. In monopoly capitalism they either do not survive or have their focus blunted.

Questions were raised about donor countries withholding aid over questions of moral or political disagreement. Jagan took issue with the motives behind such barriers. He pointed to Grenada where, while certain human rights were being denied, grass-roots democracy was developing. However, public pressure against the oppression of workers is necessary. Jagan stated that giving aid to Burnham was simply a waste of money.

The sharp declines in world sugar prices was raised for commentary by Jagan. He responded by emphasizing the need for unity among Caribbean states. Otherwise they can become the victims of exploitation by the multinationals.

As an example of exploitation, Jagan made reference to the evidence that only about 4-6 percent of the total net income from Guyana's bauxite production goes back to Guyana. He stressed the need for an integrated, co-ordinated approach among bauxite producers.

Michael Bradfield (Economics, Dalhousie University, Halifax) concentrated upon the questions of government finance and foreign exchange. He said that the condition of so little of the bauxite revenue going to Guyana bears a resemblance to conditions in Atlantic Canada. Newfoundland gets more in liquor and cigarette taxes than it does in forest tax revenues. This indicates a problem of dependent areas. Financial dependency develops because of confusion, institutions, and the stupidity and rigidity of politicians and other groups in the society.

He pointed out the confusion associated with the words *investment* and *capital*. Although many people use these words simply to refer to financial transactions, their meanings involve much more. *Investment* and *capital* relate to an economy's productive capability. A debate over the priority for investment pits current consumption against additions to productive capacity.

In Nova Scotia, the major increase in provincial expenditures has been in debt payments. Foreign inflows of funds do not necessarily expand productive capability. There is no guarantee that an inflow of foreign dollars will do a country any good. This view is of course contrary to the beliefs of the current Progressive Conservative government.

Foreign money, Bradfield said, is only good to buy foreign products. Internally you still use your domestic currency. Economic stimulation occurs elsewhere.

According to Bradfield, we reach a problem once this confusion on foreign inflows is dealt with—the only possible explanation for national or provincial lust for foreign investment is the stupidity or dishonesty of politicians.

Bradfield suggested that in Nova Scotia there is too much reliance on foreign funds and too much concern about credit ratings. Problems result. When, for example, Nova Scotia sells bonds in New York, in the long run it simply ends up keeping its interest rates up, inflating the value of its currency and hurting its exports. It is dangerous to simply bring in as much foreign capital as possible and, therefore, caution should be applied to the assumed need for foreign investment. Very often this "need" simply serves the branch plants and the foreign multinationals.

Bradfield argued that often Nova Scotia has the capital but fails to look hard at its real options. He used Halifax Shipyards and Hawker Siddeley as examples. These companies had different interests than the province. Nonetheless, provincial restructuring efforts for the shipyards appear belatedly and without forcing the companies involved to act other than in their own self-interests.

All too often we overlook local products and instead import funds to buy foreign-made equipment. Unemployment is squandered savings. The real danger is long-term financial and technological dependence on others.

Question Period: A question was raised on the impact of having debts in one's own currency. **Bradfield** said that such a case (for example, Nova Scotia selling bonds redeemable in Canadian but not U.S. dollars) means that the lenders believe you really will generate an export surplus. This would be a more healthy situation.

Jagan raised the example of socialist states where bills or debts to other countries are often paid off in domestic products. He stressed that this would be against the spirit of capitalism.

Abstract of Paper Presented

Anthony Gonzales: *EEC Multilateral Aid and the Lomé Caribbean: Problems and Perspectives*

(Anthony Gonzales is with the Institute of International Relations, University of the West Indies, St. Augustine, Trinidad)

Even though the professional development community has become more skeptical over the last two decades about the efficiency of aid in promoting development, there is still a substantial measure of agreement on the fact that as far as small countries are concerned, aid under appropriate conditions is an indispensable element in the development process.

In their efforts at structural transformations, Caribbean economies are faced with the serious bottlenecks of low capital formation, inadequate foreign-exchange earnings, technological insufficiency, and lack of technical skills. Contrary to expectations in the 1960s, aid has become in the 1980s a critical input for augmenting domestic savings, particularly public savings, and a necessary means for procuring essential imported supplies. This is especially the plight of the non-oil economies of the region, for whom transformation has now become a monumentally superhuman task.

In elaborating their development plans and perspectives, Caribbean countries have always sought to develop strategies and policies aimed at increasing the trade and aid opportunities available to the region. Although a significant degree of market access and commodity protection for some traditional export crops has been achieved, the export sector has not shown the dynamism that was anticipated. On the contrary, severe downturns in export performance have been such that external capital flows are now perceived as having equal if not more importance than trade.

The Lomé trade and aid pact represented a major breakthrough in North-South relations for the Caribbean. However, it entered into force at the very beginning of the world oil crisis, and its implementation occurred simultaneously with falling raw material prices and soaring terms-of-trade losses for the non-oil Caribbean countries. By the end of the first Lomé convention, the average Caribbean state, which had entered the Lomé agreement emphasizing protection for sugar, bananas and rum and the broadening of trade opportunities, found external capital assistance to be more critical to its development.

The modest objectives of the Caribbean in the negotiations of the Lomé financial arrangements centred mainly on increasing the volume of assistance for the smaller least-developed countries of the region and generally improving the quality of and control over aid commitments and disbursements.

In the main, the Lomé arrangement comprises three forms of assistance. The first is project aid related to national and regional indicative programs and geared to cover activities in investment and technical-assistance programs in development plans. It is 78 percent of total aid. The second is compensatory program assistance related to transfers for the decline in export earnings as well as difficulties connected to a decline in production. These are the resources allocated to stabilization of export earnings (STABEX) and constitute approximately 15 percent of total resources. The third is emergency aid, which is about 4 percent and used for relief operations.

These three types of assistance, while useful in the past, today do not reflect the significant changes that have occurred in the needs of Caribbean states for assistance. With the present foreign-exchange crisis, a new range of projects and programs necessary to the development of the region is now available for financing. The concentration on project financing appears to seriously limit the possible use of European Development Fund (EDF) resources under these circumstances. It is also evident that a program of balance-of-payments support is required on an emergency basis in light of the economic collapse in the several Caribbean states that have been most seriously affected by the deterioration of the world economic situation. This support is essential if these countries are to maintain even their present levels of imports.

Trends and Prospects

The world economic crisis that started in 1973 and worsened in 1980-83 produced a sizable demand for external financing in the region. Rough estimates would indicate that the Lomé Caribbean countries now need US$2-2.5 billion to meet the external resource gap and to generate moderate growth rates over the next five years.

Although the Caribbean received an increased flow of concessional capital, this was not sufficient to offset the significant terms-of-trade losses and the appreciable decline in non-concession flows.

The impact of the terms-of-trade losses on small, higher-income developing countries is just as disastrous as it is on poorer countries. As small economies remain dependent on one or two primary export crops, a fall in the basic price of an export crop occasions a huge drop in foreign exchange, which seriously affects the capacity of these economies to attract non-concessionary funds because their credit worthiness is impaired by the negative performance of their undiversified export sectors.

The inadequacy of the flow of capital resources to the Caribbean is tied to the failure of the developed countries to attain more appropriate targets of assistance to the developing world. The World Bank has argued for a doubling of aid to low-income countries. At the same time, the European Economic Community (EEC) member states, at the Paris conference on the least-developed states, reaffirmed their intentions to reach the 0.7 percent UN development aid target. The maintenance of these resources in real terms over the 1985-90 period by an adjustment for inflation of 6 percent would result in a calculation of ECU$13.4 billion for this period.

Concern about the fluctuations and the uncertainty surrounding the availability of community financial resources has always been expressed by the African, Caribbean and Pacific (ACP) countries. This, to a large extent, is related to the fact that the political will to attain the UN target of 0.7 percent of gross national product (GNP) is weakening as EEC official development aid (ODA) assistance is stagnating around 0.46 percent of GNP because of serious reservations about the capacity to increase these flows to developing countries.

The EEC Commission, in its effort to introduce a larger degree of automaticity and predictability in EEC resource flows to developing countries, has suggested that if the Community set 1 percent of its GNP as its aid target for attainment over the next ten years, then Community aid would increase by 16 percent. It can be observed that if the Community attains the 1 percent target by the year 2000, there would be a 7 percent annual increase in total Community ODA, assuming that GNP grows at 2 percent annually over this period. Since Lomé resources represent approximately 5 percent of total Community ODA, this could mean an increase of actually disbursed aid from 600 million European Units of Account (EUA) in 1980 to about 2,100 billion EUA by the year 2000.

The prospects for achieving any of these criteria remain very dim in the present state of tight budgeting, semirecovery in Europe and widespread aid fatigue. Even though ACP-EEC relations have their own dynamics, are of an historically special nature and continue to reflect expanding areas of mutual advantage and interdependence, most realistic predictions, as the current negotiations demonstrate, would suggest that maintaining Lomé II resources in real terms would not be an insignificant ACP achievement. As for the implications for the Caribbean, it would appear that an appropriate complementary strategy would be to seek more suitable ways of attracting non-concessionary EEC capital through existing and modified Lomé arrangements.

TECHNOLOGY AND MANAGEMENT
IN DEVELOPMENT

Summary of Presentations

by Chairperson Phil Thompson

Jacqueline Archer (Information Specialist, Caribbean Industrial Research Institute, Trinidad) stressed the information gaps that exist between developed and developing countries. She said information from the developed world is not properly adapted to local realities. An indigenous infrastructure is needed to perform this translation and to co-operate with external-aid or corporate actors.

She felt that buying hard technology from the developed world is a mistake, that the know-how to produce such technology locally is more important. Many errors occur in the Caribbean because purchasing skills—the ability to evaluate available products—are poorly developed.

She said that, to better control foreign exchange, improved alternatives to existing technology suppliers must be developed. She suggested that joint ventures with European partners could be valuable, but outlined how often the management costs exceed the scale of projects, hinting that too much luxury is built into foreign-controlled projects. She referred to the Mexican state technology-initiatives registry as a good example of how to avoid "reinventing the wheel."

Yassin Sankar (Management, Dalhousie University, Halifax) spoke about his research in the Caribbean based on the transfer of management technology. He said that, without the transfer of appropriate management skills, all other transfers of technology will inevitably fail. He claimed there is much mismanagement in the Caribbean and that this contributes to economic problems there.

He said that the tools of information processing and decision-making common to North American firms and transnational corporations operating in the Caribbean are not used by indigenous firms. He discussed what he called the "tools of management" and described how few of these modern management tools were used by subjects interviewed in the region. The diffusion of management practices was very low, except within multinationals.

He had studied the diffusion process of management innovation and again had found little communication or adoption of management tools by his targets in the Caribbean. He analysed the factors that inhibit such diffusion and provided a list of 24 items that limit adoption of modern management tools.

Sankar hinted that Caribbean ideology mitigates against management practices as we define them in North America, and he made several recommendations for change, among them that: (1) Caribbean businesses undertake performance audits and include job design in this initiative, (2) Caribbean businesses seriously study manpower planning and (3) training programs should be developed for high-level management.

During the question period several Caribbean participants voiced their concern that the study may be culturally biased, and referred to Ms. Archer's claim that management costs of projects seem to be too high, perhaps because of the very complexity suggested by Sankar.

Harvey Silverstein (President, Maritime Technology Consultants Ltd., Halifax), who has worked widely in the Caribbean, spoke of the importance of assessment in the transfer of technology. He expressed concern about the doers and victims in technology transfer. He cited cases in which an understanding of sociology and anthropology could have prevented disastrous transfers of technology. In one case, the provision of outboard motors had destroyed the fabric of coastal communities by expanding the natural boundaries of inshore fishermen. He said the impact of technology upon communities must be analysed in advance to prevent this sort of disruption. Technology doesn't have to evolve to meet Third World problems but just has to be applied appropriately. Mr. Silverstein said obsolete technologies are being transferred too often without the means for their service and repair.

He said two-way trade and exchange is critical because we have much to learn from Caribbean countries; giveaways are harmful and should be stopped because they lower self-respect. We should remember that innovation and entrepreneurs go hand in hand, so small-scale, private-sector activity should be fostered where possible.

Tom Nickerson (Nova Scotia Research Foundation Corporation, Dartmouth, Nova Scotia) spoke about the role of the Nova Scotia Research Foundation Corporation in the development of technology in Nova Scotia. He stressed the importance of technology to the Nova Scotian economy and cited the recent economic development policy statement of the provincial government. He outlined how the appropriate use of technology leads to economic competitiveness and warned that small Nova Scotia firms will be pushed out of business by pressures in the world economy unless they develop and use appropriate technology. He described a microprocessor sawmill-control product that improved the efficiency of lumbering as an example of high-tech appropriate technology.

The role of the Nova Scotia Research Foundation Corporation is to do research into technologies to generate economic wealth (they have performed 4,000 research projects for 600 companies). Companies must generate business from its research activities and survive on their own.

He was very interested in discussion about the Caribbean because of the similarities between that region and Atlantic Canada.

EMPLOYMENT AND UNEMPLOYMENT

Summary of Presentations

by Dan MacInnes

David Abdulla (Secretary-Treasurer, Oil Field Workers Trade Union, Trinidad and Tobago) said that the trade union he represents started in a "national explosion" of labour unrest in the oil fields. British troops put down the insurrection of June 1937 by killing nineteen persons and injuring many more.

Unemployment in the Caribbean is a structural problem. The official estimate is that 15-16 percent of the labour force in Trinidad and Tobago is unemployed, compared with Jamaica's 40 percent. However, as in other places, these figures do not represent those who have stopped looking for work, those who are underemployed or those who are only seasonally employed. Even in boom times, the unemployment rate went down only to 11 percent.

Outside control of the economy and the resultant corporate objectives cause constant fluctuations because the key sectors are primary products–oriented and without backward and forward linkages. Oil, sugar, bananas, etc. are developed or held back according to world commodity prices and markets.

The heavy investment of government in construction projects to increase primary production for export (steel and fertilizers) led to a rapid expansion and subsequent collapse of the labour sector, to deficit financing by government and to cutbacks in social services.

Now half the trade-union movement is on strike, with serious political ramifications.

Richard Cashin (President, Newfoundland Fishermen, Food and Allied Workers Union, St. John's) noted that the situation in Newfoundland is similar to that in Trinidad and Tobago. He spoke on the smugness of Atlantic Canada towards labour. Newfoundland, however, is becoming more aware. Change is taking place. Newfoundland used to send poor-grade fish to Trinidad and, in turn, Trinidad sent its lowest-grade rum to Newfoundland. Both places are united in their underdevelopment. Newfoundland has the highest unemployment rates in Canada and, like Trinidad, its trade-union movement was founded in 1937. Half the members are also on strike now.

Cashin said that a certain romanticism rationalizes that, because it is so great to be a Newfoundlander, the cost of unemployment and underemployment is made bearable. This mystique is encouraged by politicians and professors who are committed to the status quo and see workers' demands as threatening to a "cherished way of life."

The lines are being drawn in Newfoundland. For the first time since Confederation, the labour movement is creating a new consciousness. People are going to jail, injunctions are being put in place, police are at the picket lines "enforcing the law," and teachers and churches are becoming radicalized.

Dependency can be turned on its head if workers say, we don't need these conditions of work, take your company and go, we don't need it.

Farley S. Brathwaite (Government and Sociology, University of the West Indies, Cave Hill, Barbados; abstract of paper follows), in agreement with Abdulla's remarks, noted a continuing increase in unemployment in the Caribbean. He said that the official rate of unemployment depends on the official definition of unemployment. There is clear evidence to indicate that unemployment in the Caribbean is seriously underestimated. His own research indicates that actual unemployment rates may well be three times the official figures.

Brathwaite said that unemployment results from the type of economy existing in the West Indies.

The policy initiatives of government were presented in their respective guises—modernization programs related to job training, and incentive programs to create manufacturing jobs. The actual jobs in manufacturing were generally half of those initially promised. Generated jobs also are associated with a certain number of lost jobs.

Respecting tourism, the promise of jobs and the strategy of supporting the private sector as the initiator of these jobs were seen as similar to those in manufacturing. There is a surge of employment followed by a steady loss of jobs. However, there may be indirect employment (in the informal sector—beach bums, street artists, etc.).

The skills-training program (a modernization approach) involves few people, and then only about one-half of those actually trained are placed in existing jobs. These programs have failed because they are used for political rather than economic purposes, they are a consequence of business "needs" that fluctuate widely, and they exist within an environment of abundant, cheap labour.

Robert Hill (Sociology, Memorial University, St. John's, Newfoundland) began with two empirical observations: (1) Atlantic Canada has higher rates of unemployment than the rest of Canada, but most theories of unemployment do not relate to the rural sector, and (2) there are significant differences in the conditions of unemployment in the metropolitan and rural areas.

Agreeing with Brathwaite, he said the official statistics do not tell us much about the actual conditions of unemployment, and real unemployment appears to be three times the official rate.

In rural areas, the new phenomenon is that the deviant is the person with work. The whole question of *employment* needs to be re-examined, given the fact that unemployment is the rural reality rather than the reverse as people commonly assume to be the case.

Hill argued that training programs in high unemployment areas are of little use to the real economy and recommended that rural areas abolish all unemployment "retraining" programs and give the money to local communities (e.g., in the form of quotas, crown lands and mineral rights).

Phil Thomson's question: Isn't rural life cheaper, and isn't rural unemployment qualitatively different? Hill's answer: No, Newfoundland is not Nova Scotia. Why should teachers get pay plus subsistence while fishermen do not? The experience in Trinidad is the same—the informal economy doesn't do everything.

Abstract of Paper Presented

Farley S. Brathwaite: *Unemployment in Barbados: A Preliminary Analysis of Selected Policy Programs*

(the full text of this paper can be found in a companion volume to this publication, *Rethinking Caribbean Development*)

The reduction of unemployment is a major objective of development, and the purpose of this paper is to outline, examine and analyse selected policy approaches to unemployment in Barbados.

Broadly speaking, the policy approaches to unemployment can be classified under four headings:

1. *Job-creation strategies*, such as industrial development, tourism development and public works programs, directed at increasing the demand for labour.
2. *Training programs* directed at increasing the supply of appropriately trained labour.
3. *Job counselling, recruitment and placement programs* directed at matching labour to available jobs.
4. *Social-security measures* to ease the financial burden of those displaced from the employed labour force through unemployment.

Data show that jobs have been created, job-seekers have been trained, recruited and placed locally and overseas, and programs have been set in place to make provisions for some of those displaced through unemployment. Notwithstanding this, there is evidence that job-creation strategies have not lived up to expectations, and it is widely accepted that the training, recruitment, placement and unemployment-benefit schemes have suffered a similar fate.

Conclusions with respect to *job-creation strategies* in manufacturing and tourism are somewhat limited because of the methodological difficulty in estimating indirect job creation. Notwithstanding this, the evidence on direct employment in the manufacturing sector suggests that the impact of this strategy has been limited by the capital-intensive nature and limited labour-absorptive capacity of these operations. Furthermore, there are indications that the more highly developed manufacturing sector, with its more favourable wage structure and apparently more secure and attractive employment opportunities, has had an underdeveloping effect on agriculture and independent self-employment. Given the fly-by-night nature of some manufacturing operations, many of these jobs have been essentially short-term, temporary and uncertain.

Similar observations can be made about the limited capacity for employment generation in the tourism sector. The tourism sector has been far less labour-intensive than predicted, with an unexpectedly low level of labour absorption. The impact of tourism on employment tends to be short-term and temporary, given the seasonal nature of tourism and because the boom period in job creation and employment is short-lived. Furthermore, the jobs created are largely unskilled, and the more desirable jobs, especially in the multinational hotels, which account for the larger part of the sector, may be going to expatriates. As with the manufacturing sector, it can be argued that this sector may not improve the overall employment situation because, although it creates jobs, it also has a tendency to close jobs in other sectors, including agriculture.

With respect to *training strategies*, the extent to which these will affect unemployment depends on the wage structure, the availability of jobs, the availability of appropriate jobs, and the willingness of training-program graduates to accept any jobs which may be available. Besides the non-availability of jobs, there are other features of the scheme which may adversely affect its implementation. For example, training-program instructors are reportedly unhappy with having to carry out a placement function and feel that graduates are not as prepared as they should be, a view which popular opinion suggests is shared by employers as well.

With respect to *placement services*, the overseas placement scheme did place relatively large numbers. However, these jobs are basically short-term and temporary. This scheme also runs into conflict with the training scheme. For example, in 1978, the year of the introduction of the skills-training program to alleviate "the shortage" of skilled labour, the overseas-placement program placed 132 carpenters, 172 masons, 45 mechanics, 31 plumbers, 14 electricians and 9 joiners in the farm-labour scheme in the USA and Canada.

With respect to local placement schemes, the inavailability of sufficient and appropriate jobs makes placement problematic.

The picture of the policy approaches that emerges is characterized by: (1) low levels of job creation, (2) the creation of jobs that are largely temporary, short-term and unattractive with respect to salary and conditions of service, (3) the creation of jobs that may actually represent a transfer of labour from one sector to another rather than a creation of "real" jobs and (4) the establishment of training, registration and placement schemes that fail to have the expected impact on unemployment because of the inavailability of sufficient and appropriate jobs.

Finally, the *unemployment insurance* scheme has been very limited in its effect because it does not address the needs of all the unemployed.

In broader perspective, it can be argued that the limited impact of the strategies discussed above can best be explained in the context of the wider political economy. The dependent approach to development and employment generation has generally meant that linkages with the wider economy and self-sustaining growth have been restricted, and has resulted in the use of training programs whose viabilities have not been adequately explored in relation to Barbados. It has given rise to an inordinate emphasis on profit maximization and on providing generous financial incentives, including cheap labour, to foreign capital.

For all intents and purposes, the programs have been short-term and ad hoc, rather than part of long-term comprehensive planning. They have emerged mainly in response to cyclical crises in the economy and society. It can be argued that most if not all of the programs have been attempts to control political crisis and to regulate labour.

This social-control function was clearly evidenced in the context in which the program of manufacturing and tourism development emerged. It is also evidenced in the unemployment benefit scheme which, by virtue of its exclusion clauses, attempts not only to divide the unemployed into the genuinely unemployed and the "voluntarily idle" but to control labour protest by rendering those participating in industrial disputes liable to denial of unemployment benefits. The same is true of the national registration schemes, which also attempt to divide the unemployed into genuinely unemployed and "voluntarily idle" (as can be seen on page 171 of the 1983-88 national development plan, which suggests that the National Employment Bureau will help determine whether unemployment is voluntary or not).

In conclusion, the limited impact of the social policies to deal with unemployment results from a displaced emphasis in strategies.

ROLE OF NGOs IN DEVELOPMENT

Summary of Workshop and Follow-up Session

by Chairperson George Schuyler

Forty to fifty people attended the non-governmental organization (NGO) workshop, which started very late. The goal was to focus on development activities being carried out by Canadian and Caribbean NGOs and on how we might encourage closer ties. After a brief overview of Canadian activities by **Joan Campbell** of Development and Peace, Halifax, **Oscar Allen** of Projects Promotion, St. Vincent, examined the perception of development from the grass roots—what people do for themselves rather than what than what others do for them. **Marlene Greene** of Canadian University Service Overseas (CUSO) and **Bob Thompson** of Agriculture Canada commented briefly on the presentations.

Much of the discussion was taken up by a debate on the issue of why Canadian NGOs do not have more people from visible minorities on their staffs. One response was that the NGOs have progressed a great deal over the past ten years and are much more sensitive to this issue. A second comment was that development staff should be selected on the basis of competence.

Because of the lively discussion and a shortage of time, a follow-up session was held at the International Education Centre on Sunday morning. The participants discussed concrete ways to share ideas and to provide a directory of organizations in Atlantic Canada and the Caribbean to help interested people contact each other. Sharing information through newsletters and exchanges of personnel were also discussed.

The overall impact of the two NGO sessions was excellent in terms of networking.

ORGANIZING PRIMARY PRODUCERS

Summary of Presentations

by Chairperson Rick Williams

Michael Belliveau (Maritime Fishermen's Union, Nova Scotia) and **Peter deMarsh** (President, New Brunswick Woodlot Owners Association) presented excellent reviews of the current situations and histories of struggles to organize inshore fishermen and woodlot owners respectively. Both gave much relevant background information and explanation and ended with good strategies and theoretical points.

Belliveau said fishermen have achieved collective bargaining rights in New Brunswick, but in Nova Scotia and P.E.I. they do not have these rights and therefore it is difficult to establish stable, self-financing organizations in those areas. Bargaining has been difficult in New Brunswick because of the poor condition of the industry overall and the opposition of the companies. The future of the Maritime Fishermen's Union depends upon its finding financial stability through bargaining and through its involvement in marketing the underutilized species that inshore fishermen depend on.

The struggle of woodlot owners in New Brunswick, **deMarsh** said, has been successful in that it has created a viable organization that has united the disparate elements in this sector and made positive gains for them. The major concern now is with the ability of the organization to survive and adapt to changing conditions in the industry. The woodlot owners need to overcome their isolation from other producer and worker organizations, particularly the trade unions in the forest industry.

The presentation by **Marie Burge** (National Farmers Union, Prince Edward Island) on farmers had a more theoretical focus, being concerned with the class position of farmers. She analysed the difficulties in getting farmers to understand that the majority of them are neither small business operators nor capitalists. Interest costs, the pressure to use capital-intensive methods, and the control of agribusiness corporations over commodity prices, markets, farm equipment costs and so on have all kept farmers in a dependent and highly unstable position. The success of militant farm organizations, specifically the National Farmers Union, depends upon more producers realizing that they have to act collectively to defend their interests and that government-sponsored organizations and the federation approach only divide and manipulate farmers.

David Abdulla (Secretary-Treasurer, Oil Field Workers Trade Union, Trinidad and Tobago), described a range of problems affecting farm workers and small farmers in Trinidad and Tobago. Principal among these are the (1) gobbling up of the best agricultural land by speculators building housing for suburban development, (2) the displacement of local production by imported food products paid for by oil and gas revenues, (3) the decline of the traditional sugar-cane industry because of substitute products and the consequent impoverishment of cane workers, (4) floods and erosion caused by poor land-management practices and (5) the generally low incomes and social marginality of small producers. There has been some success in organizing primary producers, such as the cane workers who are in the oil-field workers' union, and in setting up alternative marketing systems and co-ops.

Discussion: There was not much time for discussion with the audience. One point of debate was whether the problems of farmers and fishermen in the Maritimes were more the result of market conditions, overproduction and other structural characteristics of these industries than the result of the specific activities of large corporations. One response in the case of fishing was that the corporations, in tandem with government, have worked to maintain overproduction and other structural distortions through a heavy push for capitalization and quantitative expansion at the expense of quality and market value.

There was an interesting discussion about strategies for linking primary producers with other working-class organizations or movements. The situation in the Maritimes was compared with that in the Caribbean, where there seems to have been more success in this regard.

ORGANIZING FOR CHANGE

Summary of Presentations

by Brian O'Neill

Barry Chevannes (Worker's Party, Jamaica) introduced his talk by suggesting a basic contradiction between imperialism and the people. He then defined two phases in recent social/political struggles in the West Indies in general, and in Jamaica in particular.

From the late 1960s to 1980, there was an upsurge in political and social militancy. A crisis in Jamaica in 1968 was triggered by the exclusion of Walter Rodney from the country. Underlying the demonstrations were social and racial tensions that had been building for some time. At the same time there were protests and riots in Trinidad that reflected similar grievances. Although the progressive movement was stymied in Grenada in 1974, a successful revolution occurred in that country in 1979.

A period of regression began in 1980 with the defeat of the Manley government in Jamaica. The U.S. invasion of Grenada in 1983 sealed the primacy of reaction in most parts of the region.

Chevannes suggested that a number of lessons may be learned from both periods:

1. Practical political experience reveals the consciousness of the people. In 1977, economic difficulties in Jamaica induced the Manley government to approach the International Monetary Fund (IMF) for financial assistance. The Left failed to convince the people that the IMF's terms should not be accepted. With the general acquiescence of the public, the government reached an agreement with the IMF that undermined the social gains of the previous five years. This ultimately led to the defeat of the Manley government. Seaga was elected on the issue of obtaining a better deal with the IMF. His election resulted in the dismantling of social programs.
2. Without dealing with the bread-and-butter issues facing people, progressive teaching about issues will not work.

3. There is the need to link the struggle for reforms within the established capitalist political order to the struggle to overthrow the system.
4. Working-class support in this struggle is the decisive element for obtaining success. Manley was succeeding before reactionary forces undermined workers' support for his government. (During the first two years of the New Jewel Movement government in Grenada, workers interests had also been neglected.)

With regard to the links the progressive petit-bourgeois intelligensia endeavours to establish with the working class, Chevannes made two points: (1) mass militancy on the part of workers is subject to the vulnerability of high unemployment, and (2) the economy as a whole in all the capitalist Caribbean countries is vulnerable because most of these countries are dependent on the operations of multinational companies, which can pull up stakes and move whenever they decide to.

Gilles Theriault (President, Maritime Fishermen's Union) suggested two main issues of development in Atlantic Canada: the organization of fisheries' workers for change in the industry, and the organization of the labour movement as a whole.

He traced his own involvement in political and social struggles in the Maritimes. He was a product of the university radicalism of the late 1960s and early 1970s, which involved various forms of protest against social injustice. From there he entered the world of work and political organizing in 1971.

"Have we made progress?" he asked rhetorically. Given his continuous efforts beginning in a fishing village in New Brunswick, are fishermen better off now than they were thirteen years ago? Has the labour movement improved? Has the economic system improved? Is there a more equitable distribution of wealth regionally, nationally and internationally? "I don't think so."

"But thirteen years is not a long time," Theriault continued. "The struggle is worth it." He, along with others, had set out to organize inshore fishermen. They ultimately convinced the New Brunswick government to grant collective bargaining to inshore fishermen. But, he argued, organizing inshore fishermen is not enough. All fishery workers—inshore, trawler, and plant workers—must be organized to change the direction of the industry and to obtain greater benefits and control.

To accomplish this end, his union has sought to establish supportive links with organized labour, with the provincial federations of labour and the Canadian Labour Congress. He is convinced that there must be one big fishery union actively linked with provincial federations of labour in order for the struggle of fishery workers to be successful.

He stated that union leadership, in general, is detached from the rank-

and-file membership. For example, although organized labour formally supports the New Democratic Party (NDP), the rank and file does not. Labour leadership tends to sweep this anomaly under the rug. The one activity that does not involve the rank and file of the labour movement is the collective bargaining process. Theriault concluded that rank-and-file involvement must be increased here in order to deal with larger political and social issues.

David Abdulla (Secretary-Treasurer, Oil Field Workers Trade Union, Trinidad and Tobago) approaching the topic from a syndicalist point of view, initiated his remarks by saying that, unless labour holds the reins of power and the people own the country's resources, full development cannot be realized. The working class in the Caribbean has always been in the forefront of social and political struggles, particularly since the 1920s.

During the 1940s, influenced by the Westminster, two-party parliamentary model of democracy, the middle class started to take over the leadership of political movement in the Caribbean. From the mid-1950s there has been a significant outburst of militancy among workers' movements on the average of once every five years. But this militancy has often been stifled by union leaderships. The leaders have divided their members, while also regulating and minimizing conflicts. This has occurred in many unions where democracy is at a low level.

Abdulla raised the important question of how the Left intelligensia can communicate with workers but did not propose an answer. He concluded by saying there is a profound political and economic crisis in the Caribbean today. He warned that right-wing forces would like to form fascist movements to galvanize popular disenchantment.

Alexa McDonough (Leader, Nova Scotia New Democratic Party) introduced her talk by noting that 57 percent of Nova Scotia's wealth is owned by 1 percent of the population. She used this statistic and others to demonstrate that the province's present distribution of wealth is little different from what it was 20 years ago. Among other things, the local manufacturing industry is owned by extraprovincial interests. This political and economic situation of dependence has tended to produce intellectual poverty among ruling elites in the province.

Given this situation, the NDP set up 20 study groups around Nova Scotia a few years ago to generate ideas regarding economic development. It has been a frustrating exercise but worthwhile. Without qualifying that remark, McDonough went on to explain how these study groups operated.

Instituting and activating the groups was a four-stage process: (1) discussion papers dealing with the present stage of provincial economic development were prepared and distributed, (2) individuals having influence or leadership at grass-root levels were recruited, (3) these leaders, in turn, recruited other people to participate in the study groups, which then met for discussions over a ten-week period, and (4) people were assembled to discuss case studies at a provincewide conference.

The major consensus was that there must be a higher degree of local control and participation in decision-making regarding economic development issues. McDonough concluded that more radical approaches to development are not possible until popular consciousness changes.

Discussion: Although there was little time available for discussion following these presentations, **Bob Buckingham** (business representative for the Public Service Alliance of Canada [PSAC] in Gander, Newfoundland) made observations that seemed to gain wide concurrence. He noted that, given the subject of the workshop, "Organizing for Change," there had been insufficient focus on some of the significant political movements that have developed in recent years in Canada. Specifically, he referred to the women's movement, and to the formation of solidarity coalitions initiated in British Columbia and continued in Alberta and, more recently, in Newfoundland. He said that, although he himself works for a union, he felt that most of the speakers had placed too much emphasis on the primacy of unions and the organized working class in effecting social change.

LOCAL GOVERNMENT INITIATIVES

Transcripts of Presentations

Ron McDonough: *Local Government Initiatives*

(Ron McDonough is the Policy Planner, New Brunswick Department of Commerce and Development)

Perhaps the best way to introduce these programs is to give you a comparative introduction on some common economic problems facing the Atlantic Provinces and the Caribbean. I am not suggesting that these are exactly parallel conditions, because they are not. I am suggesting that they are generally comparable conditions and that some of the initiatives I would like to discuss here may have some relevance to development at the local level in countries such as Jamaica.

Mr. Manley gave a very impressive speech as usual last night. He stressed the difficulties of achieving economic development in a primary or resource-based economy. Very simply put, the money is in manufacturing or processing, typically, in terms of the value added to products, etc. When one is forced to rely on primary industries, the raw material base, some very severe parameters are imposed on how far development can proceed, at least at the local level. He presented this as a very common problem in the West Indies and discussed various initiatives and directions for getting into manufacturing and processing to achieve some sort of independence.

Very similar conditions exist in the Atlantic Provinces—in New Brunswick, for example, despite the fact that we started out as the boom area of Canada in the nineteenth century and controlled a very healthy shipbuilding and manufacturing industry. As time went on, iron ships came along, our customers managed to take over production of those, and we went out of business. Centralist policies, in the national focus of Canada at that time, which I am not going to go into in any detail, also tended to deflect attention from development efforts in this area. To make a long story short, we continue to have a very strong reliance on primary industries in New Brunswick. Although we still have some strong areas, such as pulp and paper processing, we do not have an as well-developed industrial manufacturing base as one would hope.

At the same time, there has been a general consensus in a lot of development theory, applied theories at least, that if you are going to go into these areas, the big-boom approach is a very risky one. You don't go holus-bolus into the establishment or try to attract huge multinational enterprises into regions without being aware that you are taking a hell of a risk, because they can leave tomorrow morning. They are there for the money and that is it.

I think it has been generally accepted that if one can foster entrepreneurs at the local level, particularly in more modest types of business enterprises, small businesses in particular, this may develop a localized, perhaps locally interested, economic base with its various spinoffs. So the focus of our department has been on smaller enterprises, and the hope is that they will bring about a more profitable development situation than currently exists.

Let me review two initiatives in operation in New Brunswick that will be of the most interest to you. (I should add that a lot of other programs are provided by the government—information, analytical support staff, etc.—but these are more direct subsidy programs.)

The first program, the Small Industry Financial Assistance Program (SIFAP), was initiated in 1973 and was the first in Canada of its type. It was jointly funded by the federal and provincial governments and started as a pilot project in the northeastern region of the province. It has proved to be initially quite successful, and by 1980 it was expanded to the entire province. Funding this fiscal year will approach $5 million. Although the initial focus was on processing and manufacturing, it has been expanded to certain other areas that seem to have some entrepreneurial capacity. For example, tourism has recently been given consideration for this program.

The program funds small businesses, principally in the processing and manufacturing fields, which cannot have sales in excess of $1.5 million a year. It is restricted to relatively small outfits. They can use it to set up a business, to expand an existing one, to develop certain facilities for repair, etc., provided they fall within these major guidelines.

Provided matching dollars (50-cent dollars or whatever you want to call them) have been thus far well taken up and quite successful if one compares the investments against the capital development that has been achieved. Since 1973 there have been 869 projects funded—everything from bakers to makers of concrete forms and small manufacturing enterprises—at a cost of about $17.2 million, which we think translates into roughly 4,000 jobs, joined with a capital investment by companies of about $46 million over the same period.

One of the primary objectives of the program was to create employment, an obvious goal of development. It has been felt that this type of small-venture approach has a much greater success rate in producing jobs and viable long-term opportunities than large, big-boom sorts of adventures. The objective has been to encourage and assist the establishment of new small industries and the modernization and expansion of existing small industries in New Brunswick.

Again, to be eligible the business must be located in New Brunswick, must be involved in processing and manufacturing (except the new exceptions that show promise), and gross sales cannot exceed $1.5 million. If they have previously received assistance, the aggregate of proposed financial assistance can not exceed $75,000. Rolling stock, on-road vehicles, mobile operations and that sort of thing have not been eligible under the program, but it does cover a wide range of industries—machine shops; bakeries; pre-cast, pre-stressed concrete; and on and on. Generally it has been judged a success and we are hoping the initiative will continue to generate small businesses at the local level.

The second program is called the Venture Capital Support Program (VCSP). This one is a little more complicated—if I make some mistakes, please bear with me. Although we were the leader with our SIFAP program, which has been copied by many other jurisdictions, we are a follower with this program. Many other jurisdictions in Canada have tried this idea and, based on what appears to be a fair amount of success, we have entered into it as well. But it is a brand new program so I can't evaluate its success in New Brunswick for you. The purpose of this program, unlike the direct subsidies of the small industry program, is to encourage general entrepreneurial investment in the province.

I guess the program rests on the assumption that in Canada there appears to be a tendency to avoid risk capital and to put money into very safe, cosy investments such as Canada Savings Bonds. That type of investment does not really help the province very much. So this program is an attempt to encourage people who have small amounts of money they would normally put into savings to invest in venture-capital institutions that in turn will invest in small businesses, the same kind of enterprises I was talking about under the SIFAP program. Once again, manufacturing and processing tend to be the driving areas of concern. It is a little more complicated because you are going one step away from the businessman himself. The program is designed to encourage the formation of investment capital for industrial growth, to encourage diversification of the industrial base of the province and to encourage an improvement in the debt and equity position of the province.

The VSCP provides an interest-free loan made by Provincial Holdings Limited (which represents the province) to a venture-capital firm which proposes an investment in an operating company. So it generates risk capital for these small enterprises. The operating company must be an eligible company under the program, and the firm must meet certain criteria to be eligible. The loan will be equal to 50 percent of the amount of the investment to be made by the venture capital firm to the operating company. So it is a 50 percent interest-free loan that has to be made at the time of the venture-capital firm's investment in the operating company. The loan will be interest free for the first five years, during which capital repayment in part or full may be made but is not required. Interest must be paid quarterly on the decreasing balance at 50 percent of the then provincial lending rate beginning at the start of the sixth year. Interest must be paid quarterly on the decreasing balance of the loan at the full provincial lending rate beginning at the start of the seventh year. So you have money free for the earlier period, then you start paying back and then finally repayment of the loan in full must be made by the end of the ninth year.

Investments that fund the establishment or expansion or working-capital requirements of small to medium-sized New Brunswick companies for use in New Brunswick are eligible for assistance under the program. The definition, "small to medium-sized firms," allows a slightly larger operation than the SIFAP program. Small to medium-sized firms are defined as those which, at the time of the investment by the venture-capital firm, have annual sales not exceeding $5 million. Venture-capital firms can seek assistance for investments in operating companies whose principal activity is manufacturing or processing, or maintenance or repair relating to the manufacturing sector, or in other areas seen as having potential for entrepreneurial development, such as the knowledge and information development business, high-tech stuff and all sorts of stuff, if their products are primarily market-oriented. The principal activity can be the provision of tourist and related facilities. Agriculture is another area they are trying to get people into. The only eligible form of investment by the venture-capital firm and operating company is common shares, preferred shares and non-interest-bearing subordinated loans.

The venture-capital firm is eligible for assistance if it is incorporated, involved in making equity investments in other firms at a minimum shareholders' equity of $50,000, is registered with Provincial Holdings

Limited as a venture-capital firm, and maintains an equity base equal to at least twice the average amount of any assistance, due to the complexity that receives under the VSCP for matched investments. Finally, none of its shares may be owned by federal, provincial or municipal governments. There are also provisions to make sure an arms-length relationship is maintained between the holding companies, the venture-capital firms and the companies being invested in.

Despite the apparent complexity, the idea is obviously to encourage people to take a risk, to put their money into something and to have that in turn invested in businesses which hopefully will generate some good, solid, locally developed activities and ultimately some long-range employment.

There is some concern over how this program will work in New Brunswick. One of the primary areas of concern, expressed to me at least, is that there are not that many local venture-capital firms in the province. Presumably, applications will be coming from a lot of firms from outside the province. There is concern with outside forces again handling money locally, etc. However, if the money is being invested in a local firm, perhaps the presence of outside forces will not be such a significant variable. We will just have to wait and see.

Ralph Henry: *Local Government Initiatives*

(Ralph Henry teaches economics at the University of the West Indies, St. Augustine, Trinidad)

I want to make my remarks in the context of the discussion we had last night. I think everybody here agrees that Michael Manley presented a very down-to-earth, clear and heartfelt analysis of his experience in the transformation process in Jamaica. In his way of reconceptualizing the issues of development it became clear to me that what we have been doing in the Caribbean and are doing elsewhere in the world, perhaps in the Atlantic Provinces, is applying partial leadership rather than overall strategies that deal with the fundamental issues.

We in the Caribbean have experienced the failure of partial initiatives. Michael Manley last night was telling what we in the Caribbean know, that we have toyed with the export-led strategy by trying to get foreign capital to come and develop, thinking that foreign capital will come in and do the job for us, that the developing of our economies would generate the exports and export earnings we require for continued development, even for basic consumption. When that strategy ran out of steam, and it did quite quickly, we embarked on the import-substitution strategy.

We have been playing around with both strategies since then, except possibly in the case of Trinidad, where a clear initiative was taken in the early 1970s to embark on a resource-based strategy where we would diversify the economy through the conversion of oil and gas into a whole range of products. These products would, of course, be sold in the international market, because the Caribbean region represents a market of only about 5 million people, which is just the size of a city really. Our countries have always been concerned with export markets, and in any strategy we have to be concerned with exports. So Trinidad and Tobago once attempted to apply a new strategy, a direct, resource-based strategy on the basis of state capital.

I want to address this question of partial initiatives in the context of the structure of plural societies. I want to emphasize that most Caribbean societies are plural in nature. Looking at development from the perspective of plural societies, one can identify certain difficulties that do not attend the development thrust in more homogeneous societies. The populations of countries such as Malaysia, Trinidad and Tobago, and Guyana are internally divided on the basis of race, ethnicity, religion and what have you. That might strike a chord here in Atlantic Canada, where it appears that people feel a tremendous divide between the region and the rest of Canada, and even within Atlantic Canada there appears to be very serious division. So we have a question, development for whom? Which groups in these plural societies really benefit from growth and development?

If we are a government adopting a strategy that is supposed to lead to development, how do we ensure that development is not just simply enjoyed on an individual basis but that all groups feel they are sharing equitably in the proceeds of development? These are the essential issues that some of us are attempting to grapple with, not very successfully, but in a lot of the economic theorizing of the Left and Right these issues are downplayed or ignored.

The experience of Trinidad and Tobago illustrates the importance of grappling with these issues head on. Michael Manley showed that in the case of Jamaica the distribution of income became highly unequal, there was severe unemployment and the rich were getting richer—local capitalists benefitted to some extent from whatever industrial development had taken place. The same situation occurred in Trinidad and Tobago. By the end of the 1950s, one saw that statistically the distribution of income had become more unequal. There was growth but there was greater inequity in the society. The export and import-substitution strategies both promoted the same group of local capitalists. These strategies provided an entire force to protect them and their industries. The resource-based strategy was perhaps the first opportunity the government had to deal with the problem of distribution directly, in the development of industry through state capital. But what happened?

In Trinidad and Tobago you have a ruling party that has been in power for the last 27-28 years and derives political support mainly from the Black

African ethnic group. It saw itself as having a responsibility therefore to create opportunities for that group and even, to use a Jamaican expression, put the upper crust of white local capitalists on the manners. So the state now had oil revenues and became directly involved in productive activity. The government of Trinidad and Tobago today has a share in or owns outright maybe 50-60 companies, an overall investment of over TT$7 billion, which is something in the order of C$4-5 billion. A little more than TT$3 billion of that, about C$2 billion, almost half (in a small economy of 1.1 million people), is in the resource-based sector—oil, gas, fertilizers, steel—energy-intensive industries.

The government promoted its own group, so at the top of the state capitalist sector certain people enjoy plums of office and so on. These state capitalists have taken a position in alignment with the old capitalists as there does not seem to be any great divide in their conception of and relation to the mass base. At least there are occasions when there doesn't seem to be any divergence of view as to the role the masses and labour unions and so on are supposed to perform. There do come critical times when you see the ethnic divisions again becoming important and polarizing and so on.

So the state sector is dominated by Blacks, but that state sector has not really transformed the economy. Yes, we now have steel, we now have fertilizers, we now have urea-methanol and so on. But we are producing commodities to be sold on a world market where we are very much a price taker. The experience with steel has been really disastrous. You're a price taker in these new industries and they require a lot of capital (and some people seem to think that "capital-intensive" is the same thing as high technology or modern technology). Capital-intensive, modern technology is producing commodities that are selling no differently than sugar or cocoa or coffee. We are not producing goods for quickly growing markets, where the country will earn a tremendous amount of foreign exchange now that the high prices have fallen. So the new sector created by this resource strategy is not going to deliver us into the world of diversified, transformed economy with all kinds of links, generating the tremendous foreign exchange that would allow us to enjoy the high standard of living people became accustomed to during the boom years.

Now that oil prices have fallen, the country has come full-swing back to the Caribbean fold. In 1972-73, I worked for the government of Trinidad and Tobago and was involved in a frantic exercise at the end of 1972 trying to identify things to ban. It is a memory that will be with me as long as I live. We were trying to identify the things to ban because our foreign-exchange position was not better than that of most of the countries in the capitalist Caribbean today. Then we had foreign exchange to supply maybe two or three months of imports—a serious problem of foreign exchange. The government itself had no revenues and did not anticipate revenues to pay public servants and was suggesting to the oil companies and the sugar company, which was then in private hands, that they should pay taxes a little ahead of schedule to help the cash-flow problem. That was 1973. In 1983 the government of Trinidad and Tobago had to introduce measures to control the use of foreign exchange, introducing a massive bureaucratic system. We do not stop selling foreign exchange; he just said that we have to ration foreign exchange and we have to look and make all these applications for foreign exchange. But this is really the same thing we were planning to do in 1973.

What happened in 1973 was that suddenly oil prices rose and we had a tremendous amount of foreign exchange. Oil had delivered us for some time and we enjoyed very high levels of living and so on. But now, we are back into the Caribbean fold, with serious problems of foreign exchange, serious deficits in the government's budget and so on.

We want to encourage foreign investment back into the country—that's the basic strategy now being suggested by the government, because the resource-based strategy has not taken up the slack. Again there will be dependence on foreign capital.

At first the government of Trinidad and Tobago seemed very lukewarm about the whole idea of the Caribbean Basin Initiative (CBI), understood its political implications, etc., but finally it walked in very quietly, bowing gracefully and attempting to have discussions with Washington on the CBI. Of course the local capitalist class has gotten into the act again, talking about the virtues of the marketplace and so on. Now that the government faces problems of deficits and so on, there is much talk of selling off some of the enterprises now under government control—with certain implications of course, because, in an ethnically divided, plural society, one has to be concerned with how the distribution of income and wealth will determine the basic social structure of that society.

With the government attempting to take a back seat, encouraging foreign capital and promoting local private capital, we are going to see ourselves returning to the same situation that existed in the 1960s and 1970s. During the boom years those in the private sector were on their manners, so to speak. They very quietly amassed a substantial amount of capital, which allowed some of these local capitalists to become conglomerates. The previous prime minister once referred to their growth as a proliferation of sharks—they become sharks in the local environment. In the private sector, small commercial houses had become large operations by buying from abroad and selling locally. During the boom years and the period of import substitution they brought the things in completely knocked down and assembled and sold them—that was called manufacturing. That was one step removed from their basic commission agency kind of work. They become large and they have been spreading their tentacles not just within the Caribbean but even as far as North America. Some of the large local firms in Trinidad now have offices in Miami and, I imagine, in Toronto and in other places such as New York and so on. We have within our midst some small transnationals, and one can anticipate that they may move their offices from Trinidad or wherever in the Caribbean to other locations, even to North America. So we have that problem to deal with.

Now that the government is seeking to promote private enterprise, it means that the structure of incentives will support these traditional enterprises and help them to grow even more, with certain consequences for the distribution of income and so on over time. At the same time, the new strategy requires them to control wages as in the old days that Michael Manley mentioned last night—the advantage has to be the issue of wages.

So we are returning to strategies of the 1950s and 1960s without having learned the lessons of that period and still applying partial strategies to develop and diversify economies. I am sure this all sounds very gloomy, but I think it is important for us to understand these larger issues in dealing with the transformation of small communities. Regional underdevelopment needs to be understood in the context of the wider issues of development. If we do not address the longer-term issues, where is the thing likely to lead? How hard is it for various groups to participate and to share the benefits of growth? How do we, at every stage of the way, introduce mechanisms that ensure that it is not just a trickle-down effect, where at some time in the future the benefits of growth are supposed to trickle down to the mass base? How do we ensure that people at the mass base enjoy the benefits of whatever is happening? Unless we root our structures in whatever our purpose, we will find that we have merely employed another partial strategy and experienced results that are very unflattering.

Summation Address

James Petras: *Development in the 1980s and Beyond*

(James Petras is with the Sociology Department, State University of New York, Binghamton)

We have discussed many issues, theories of development, case studies of particular economic sectors, and strategies for change. We have analysed the past and the present, and the topic suggests that now I should play the role of prophet and look towards the future. I will try to integrate some of the analysis of some of the areas discussed over the past several days and try to project this as I see it, at least into the next decade. I want to do this for three general areas: (1) class and politics, (2) the world economy and (3) U.S. policy towards the Caribbean. I think that these topics form the three-legged stool of the social-economic-political realities that have been a large part of our discussions.

Class and Politics
The first theme is the pervasiveness of free-market ideology and practice in the United States, Europe, Asia, and the Caribbean, the assumption that the market, free-enterprise emphasis on the initiative of individuals and corporate power are the mechanisms for transformation, growth and prosperity. One has only to spend some time in the so-called social democratic countries of southern Europe to get a sense of this doctrine's hegemony. It has penetrated and emptied social democracy (at least in the southern parts of Europe) of any of its welfare components. Mitterand, the architect of one-half million unemployed, Gonzales in Spain with 19 percent unemployment (and I hate to say it but workers tell me it was better under Franco, believe it or not, than it is today in terms of job security under a social democratic government—a terrible thing to hear). In Portugal, the same picture emerges.

The free-market ideology and its practices, of course, have penetrated the Caribbean and are embodied in the Seaga regime. However, this movement in the Caribbean is not ascending but already in decline, having lost its major bases of support not only among the poor but among its original constituency—the middle class, the petty bourgeoisie that looked to Seaga as the great redeemer of opportunities that existed, or which they thought existed, within capitalist society. The reason is that in Caribbean societies, private enterprise has always depended heavily on state subsidies, state protection, state stimulation and state financing. To paraphrase Lenin, the state was the shell within which private enterprise flourished. In the absence of the bourgeois state, it has shown little capacity to substitute its own dynamics for that which has been abstracted from the state. So we have the slow recognition and evolution back towards state interventionism and away from foreign corporations.

151

The most idiotic conception of development I have yet heard was found in the presentation of Ronald Reagan to the World Bank in which he attacked official lending and proposed the substitution of private enterprise. The president of the World Bank, of course, formerly with the Bank of America, knows damn well that foreign capital will not build the bridges and ports and the infrastructure and power within which private foreign capital can make a profit. Again this conception of the magic of the marketplace is leading to disaster. There has not been and will not be any private foreign capital going in and creating the conditions for its own expansion. Heavy outlays by the state are required for foreign capital to create a modicum of space for its operations.

A process of demise and an increasing class polarization are emerging from these free-market policies. This is inevitable. Accompanying this will be a cross-class coalition, not only of the working masses. Broad sectors of property groups have also been adversely affected, so one is going to see the re-emergence of traditional reformist and statist movements.

The demise of free-market policies is not necessarily going to evoke their alternative, at least in the immediate future. A revolutionary kind of movement may take place in this or that country. But it seems to me that across the Caribbean the immediate alternative is a kind of reformism and a traditional state interventionism. This is in part because of the Grenadian experience. The reformist forces will be somewhat chastised, fearful and especially prone to moderating their programs the second time around so as not to provoke a response from the United States. This cycle is in a sense a repetition of the Caribbean politics of the 1950s and 1960s. Over time this will be replaced by a new cycle of reformism and populism and conservatism, this alternating pattern that, it seems to me, will be transcended in the latter part of the decade.

In this context, increasing economic development is going to create new class-based politics. Where these conditions exist today they will become essential factors and create formidable challenges to state power. Accompanying this, the immediate perspective is of an emerging reformist nationalism, which in the middle long-term will be transcended by the emergence of class politics growing either from new movements, the transformation of the social structure within old movements or the convergence of forces setting up the basis for a new, alternative political movement. Out of this industrial and economic development, there is going to be (and has begun already) a debate over what constitutes socialism, and what socialism means in terms of the organization of society.

The issue, it seems to me, is this: Socialism has been considered fundamentally in an economic context and as an instrument for the development of the productive forces. That has been in part because of the domination of the discussion by economists concerned with the problem of development and, in particular, with the patterns of growth of the productive forces. In the immediate future I foresee that the discussions will shift towards the social relations of production, the way in which the productive forces are organized. This is going to be the context in which the issues of growth and expansion will take place: the relationship between the work and the organization of the state. There has been a great deal of myopia, considering that these issues are discussed only in the advanced capitalist countries. It seems to me that these are the issues that the new generation of workers is concerned about at the workplace.

New potentialities are emerging today, new forms of organization outside the workplace, at the places of habitation, what we might call street parliaments, outside the formal parliamentary institutions, the new women's consciousness within the workplace. The small manifestation at this conference is only symptomatic of a profound rethinking of the position of working women. The class dimension of this is very important, because we talk about women in general, and I think there are profound differences in the Caribbean in particular, that have crucial dimensions in terms of what kinds of relationships this emerging women's consciousness will take and what types of social movements it will generate with what kinds of political programs. In this sense the class dimension is essential.

Issues of exploitation and oppression are important, but it is also important for us to consider the profound movement that has emerged in the Caribbean amongst uprooted people who are not exploited at the place of production because they have not been engaged in production. One can see this in part of the revolutionary process that has taken place in Central America. Dynamic forces have grown out of the large masses of uprooted people. These people have become a vanguard of urban insurrection and have been a recruiting ground. If you combine a generational phenomena, people less than 25 years old, with people who have been uprooted, you have some of the most important ingredients that became part of the Sandinista movement and played an important role in some of the street fighting that characterized the major social and political confrontations. I see this as an important element, one to be integrated into any analysis that moves beyond talking about exploitation and oppression.

The World Economy
Shifting to look at the world economy, I can only be very brief in trying to sum up the important elements. First, I see the growth of regional centres within the Third World, particularly in dynamic countries, including within the Caribbean, new networks that will enlarge the interaction between Third World countries and the small countries of both Eastern and Western Europe. I also see growing specialization among dynamic Third World countries and small countries of the more developed world, developing specialized lines of production in high and medium levels of technology. The Third World will be moving away from simplistic dichotomies

and trichotomies and the conception of the world economy based on a centre and a so-called periphery, and towards the growth of multiple centres of accumulation. Within this process a new generation of skilled and educated workers will grow alongside the unskilled and less educated. These social and economic changes are going to lead to a redefinition of political patterns and the social relations of production. These are going to be the important ingredients in defining the struggles for socialism.

There is a growth within the Third World that is pressing. Opportunities exist for Third World countries to trade with the Hungarians, with the Swedes, with the South Koreans, with the socialist countries of Asia, with the capitalist bloc, with Holland. One has to understand that the present stagnant situation is largely the result of being locked into a bilateral relationship with the United States. Opportunities exist and, with new progressive social configurations, these opportunities can be seized. The movements of Third World countries to upgrade their technical and productive bases to move beyond labour-intensive industries and towards integrating work and schooling, as in Cuba, represent very important models. These kinds of transformations are not taking place in all Third World countries, but those which have had structural transformations and created progressive social configurations and a dynamic role for the state can begin to take advantage of these opportunities.

This process of differentiation, the pressures that exist for multiple sources of accumulation, has to be the framework within which to understand U.S. policy in the Caribbean. The USA cannot economically contain the social and economic processes taking place—the differentiation, the local accumulation, the breaking of bilateral relationships, the growing diversification—and so it attempts to reimpose through military and political means what it can no longer contain through economic instrumentalities.

U.S. Policy in the Caribbean

So we come to the basic fact about U.S. policy in the Caribbean, and to what Peter Phillips said this morning: the growing militarization of the region is the fundamental fact today above and beyond the discussion of dependency. The new reality is the enormous spending and attention the USA is giving to aid, new military bases, and close ties between security forces and its rapid deployment force in the region, preparing for new Grenadas through intervention.

This reality also has a lot to do with the so-called Caribbean Basin Initiative (CBI), which is nothing more than the warmed-over free-market policies of the 1950s. Such a big hullabaloo is made about the CBI. If you look back to what was practised in the fifties, without the labels and the drums beating and flutes tooting, essentially it is investment through invitation with a Reaganite gloss. The sequence in the 1950s was the free market, leading to social polarization, the precipitation of social movements, the People's Progressive Party (PPP) in Guyana and later the Cuban Revolution and the developments in Jamaica and Grenada, and so on. This sequence of the free market, social polarization, social movements, and progressive governments is now to be aborted through a combination of the free market with militarization. The latter is to contain the inevitable adverse fall-out from the former. Reflecting on the recent past, the USA has anticipated that the free market is going to create social polarities and injustices, so military power is being strengthened precisely to accompany these economic initiatives.

It seems to me that we have to think deeply about what this militarization means. If this militarization, penetration of security forces, and narrowing of the parameters of political action were to become a reality, it could represent an enormous problem for the Caribbean. It could mean the closing of the option of peaceful change; it might mark the end of the era in which the electoral process is a meaningful vehicle for initiating structural changes.

As I foresee it, the intervention of the USA in the Caribbean will have the effect of making certain sectors of the populist and nationalist movements more moderate, if you will, pushing them towards the centre and right and radicalizing the more progressive social movements. Some sectors will tailor their programs to accommodate the new realities, to maintain good terms with Washington, and others will deepen their mobilization and develop external ties with revolutionary centres to withstand the pressures from the north.

The current boom in the USA will dissipate—this has already started in the last several months. It will dissipate into a pattern of recession with many of the factors that stimulated expansion exacerbating the decline. The large flows of capital coming in will be the large outflows of capital going abroad. Deficits and tax payments will squeeze the growth, which will be already shrinking. Hence there will be an increasing effort by Washington to retain its position through heightened protection, military adventures and state adventures—not a lessening but an increasing militarism.

This decline in the USA's economic position also will lead to the expansion of relations between regional countries—Caribbean trade with Europe; Latin America; the Eastern European countries, particularly Hungary, Bulgaria and East Germany; and African and Asian countries. The necessity of moving out from under the USA will reinforce the internal regional forces pushing for greater global flexibility and realignment. It will weaken the countries and regimes that have been counting on piggybacking on U.S. expansion and further weaken their internal position in the social bloc of power.

Moreover, I think we can expect direct U.S. intervention in Central America, which will weaken the strategic position of the USA overall throughout the region. The prolonged nature of this war and its political cross could open greater political space for all progressive movements in the region. To paraphrase Ché Guevara, U.S. direct intervention in Central America could lead to two, three or many Nicaraguas, in particular in the Caribbean, just as the defeat in Vietnam weakened the U.S. interventionary capacity in Angola and Nicaragua.

The basic confrontation at the economic level today is with the international banks. Stark choices between bank payments and investment and development programs face all the leaders in the region. The across-the-board adverse impact of bank payments sets the stage for poly-class movements for reduced payments, especially as common economic conditions emerge in a number of countries. Broad-based alliances between all the so-called productive classes and the diverse social regimes could lead to a serious challenge to the existing dominant position of the USA. The necessary prerequisite, however, is a decided shift in the access to social power, away from the petty-bourgeois nationalists to worker and peasant-based political movements. Any confrontation with the banks requires first and foremost a change in the internal structure of a regime to provide the social backing for the political will needed to say no to the banks.

The growth of class-specific movements challenges intellectuals to move away from global categories of analysis to the class analysis of particular societies within a world historical perspective. Discussions about national developmental perspectives will increasingly give way to efforts to analyse global realities through the lenses of contending classes.

To the degree that wage/class differentiation takes place through the deepening of the market, an increasing role for the Caribbean, and the manufacturing division of labour, working-class culture will replace the diffuse cultural protests of the urban poor and set the basis for new class-based cultural and political movements. It seems to me now that the potentialities exist for this kind of revolutionary coalition to mature in the coming years, bringing together the major social movements, the place of habitation, and the intellectuals who today lack opportunities to do meaningful intellectual work linked to progressive political movements. This combination, which links together intellectual work and the struggles of workers on plantations and in factories, is just emerging. It is only a question of time before it matures.

Discussion Period

On the possibility of a U.S. invasion of Cuba: Cuba would sound the death knell for Reagan. There is no question in the mind of any Pentagon analyst worth his salt that intervention in Cuba would make the American defeat in Vietnam look like a picnic. One million Cubans are armed to the teeth and prepared for massive military confrontation. Any Pentagon official will want to consider the consequences for the military budget. The public outcry over the first 50,000 American soldiers killed, which could be within months, would weigh in heavy against that kind of intervention. It is not a question of morality; it may come to that, but I think the consequences, and I say this with great confidence, would be disastrous for the Reagan administration. Materially it could be very costly and tragic for the Cuban people, but for the American government and American people it would be a catastrophe. It could bring down the Reagan government. It would certainly lead to a very chaotic situation politically in the United States. It would be a destabilizing phenomena, and the end result would be a severe weakening of the military capacity of the United States and a profound reaction against intervention, against military budgets, such as we saw in the period from 1972 to 1978 when the military budget was slashed and U.S. public-opinion polls were riding 60-70 percent against the military.

When we talk about U.S. imperialism, it is critical to remember it is a democratic imperialism. I think that is a very important distinction to make: it is an imperialism that must acquire consent. It has to manipulate the public to a point, but ultimately it has to respond to the public, and we witnessed the contradictions between democracy and imperialism in the aftermath of the defeat in Vietnam. However, successful, non-costly imperialism, such as in Grenada and the Dominican Republic, can be sold to a public looking for victories, which have been scarce in recent years.

On U.S. intervention in Nicaragua: The USA has been using mercenaries and surrogates in its attempts to overthrow the Sandinista regime, but these have been insufficient. Building bases, getting more and more advisers there, Navy manoeuvres, having American flyers carrying on reconnaissance missions (two CIA officials are shot down this week) and so on is the pattern. In the face of growing confrontation and radicalization, Nicaragua today has a war economy. The economy is organized around the country's survival. Everyone is producing and working to defend the revolution. Meanwhile, the USA is throwing hundreds of millions of dollars into its own mobilization. The logic of this pattern is that there will be a precipitating incident that will become an alibi for Washington's intervention with troops. I think that is the direction, and it will have a destablizing impact in Washington. In Reagan's second term, I feel he will be able in his own mind to flaunt the fall-out that might occur in the subsequent election. He will feel that he can now act out his ideological fantasies of a major anti-communist victory.

This confrontation will be tragic for the people of Central America; it will become a generalized war. But as the USA becomes mired in the mountains of Nicaragua and the snipers on every street corner and rooftop, and becomes weakened by politics at home, this will open up political space elsewhere. This was the profound insight if you look at it in historical retrospect. I remember all the posters with the Guevara slogan, and a lot of people thought it was simply revolutionary euphoria. Here was a romantic revolutionary talking about all the revolutions in the world and of course he was killed in Bolivia and so it was all something of a romantic caper. In fact, if you analyse the relationship between the Vietnam War and the international apparatus of the U.S. state and its capacity to involve itself, in Angola it was not able to do it. They were not able to fund the counter-revolutionaries in 1976, they were not able to intervene in Iran where they had bank capital and oil money tied up and multibillion-dollar arm sales. And of course that was the turning point, where they began to create the Soviet bogie man and a new cold war began during the Carter administration to allow a massive military buildup, to rearticulate the capacity to intervene in the Third World. But in the meantime you had Nicaragua, Iran, Angola, the Grenadian revolution and also the events in Ethiopia, a much more ambiguous process.

On the Black Movement in the USA: It is clear from all indications that there is a profound differentiation today between Blacks and the rest of the population. Puerto Ricans are somewhat closer to the Black position, but on all questions you want to look at—on intervention in the Third World, on Reagan himself, on his policies, on intervention, on all dimensions—Blacks have come out consistently in very substantial majorities on the progressive side. And there has been increasing polarization, much more so than in the period of the riots. Today Blacks are moving to the left and Whites are moving to the right. Now, we should make distinctions and observe breakdowns here between women and men, etc., but, for the moment leaving that aside, this is reinforced in the areas of Black workers, in Detroit and the other areas where you have an organized Black working class.

The problem up till now has been the absence of political organization. The Jesse Jackson phenomena tapped something which already existed. The bourgeois press made a lot of the idea that he created it. I think the processes had been going on for a long time, and I found a particular focus and expression that unfortunately was dissipated by Mondale, which leaves a lot to be desired in terms of the interests of Blacks to mobilize behind Jackson. The fall-out between supporting Jackson and Mondale is a further indication of the sophistication of this radicalization. They are not marching now. Jackson says, shift your vote to Mondale. That is not happening. There is no great excitement. Some may hold their nose and vote for Mondale, but it is no longer a movement, it is a question of individual decisions.

The critical element is the crystallization of a national political organization that captures the movement to the left. The fact I want to stress is the structural characteristics of a substantial proportion of the Black population today incorporated in the northern urban areas, particularly in the factories. So demographic and economic structural factors are very important in shaping the type of political movement that can emerge. I don't have any particular formulas, I don't have any sense of what exists today that could crystallize. There are thousands of movements in each locale but the creation of that kind of national movement has yet to come on the scene.

On the implications of high technology for social change: It seems to me that this is a big question. The educational basis for a very sophisticated kind of economic development exists in some of the Caribbean islands. You have what is called an overeducated population, overeducated because the configurations of political and social groups that stay in the economic structures existing today have not created the basis for incorporating the increasingly educated population into a productive system commensurate with their level of education. So the potentiality exists, the labour force exists today in the Caribbean. Many Caribbean people are incorporated into very sophisticated institutions in Canada and the United States without any problem. Likewise they could be incorporated in Trinidad or Jamaica.

So the question of the new international division of labour where people talk about Third World countries specializing in labour-intensive activities and trading with the advanced capitalist high-tech countries seems to me misplaced because it presumes that the Third World's overall cultural development and educational level is somehow more adapted to labour-intensive industrialization. Cuba today has developed a computer system and is beginning to manufacture computers that will be competitive in the marketplace and will create the basis at least in one sector for diversifying the economy. It seems to me that this is one of the areas today, when we talk about economic development, where manpower potentiality exists— women power, manpower, people's power—for developing economic strategies. I think this is one of the areas that has been least taken into account.

This force is going to become increasingly politically relevant. It is going to make its mark on development strategies, on the nature of political regimes. As they become more educated, these groups are going to become a very important element in shaping political movements. They don't want just any job working anyplace for low wages. Maybe that was acceptable to their grandparents or even to their parents, but it is not acceptable today. The conditions exist today in the Third World that will allow it not to have to go through the same stages of industrialization as did the West, which is behind this mechanical model of what kinds of development are possible in the Caribbean in particular. I think there will be a jumping of stages.

Concluding Sessions

Open Forum Conclusions and Resolutions

Rethinking Development

Remarks by Chairperson James Petras

A revealing aspect of our forum was that a number of the participants representing different organizations or interests in the Maritimes and in the Caribbean had not had an opportunity during the conference itself to establish linkages, and our forum was the first opportunity they had to discover each other, so to speak, or to present a desire to find counterparts with whom they could correspond and perhaps develop some common work. So ours was mainly an exploratory session, where people defined themselves as representatives of teacher's unions, representatives of oil workers, or academics with interest in and around particular areas and issues. And so our gathering was a first attempt to provide a bridge between the participants here as a basis for further collaboration. The exchange of ideas and the establishment of collaboration could not take place in one hour. However, I think we established the basis for the first stage—the exchange of information.

Women and Development

Read by Chairperson Jean Augustine

"Whereas the idea of development has always been intended to refer to the process of increasing the level of human dignity for all people,

Whereas the means of achieving development has come to be too closely identified with the efficient production of economic wealth,

Whereas this has been accompanied by the increasing degradation of the human being,

Whereas any understanding of development must therefore address all aspects of dehumanization, the exploitation of women, classes, races, rural areas, regions, nations and the economic environment,

Whereas elements in traditional cultures that may be invaluable to real social transformation and human liberation must be recognized,

Therefore be it resolved that:

1. Any conference on development must address all the above issues, and the issues of female exploitation and degradation must be given full attention,

2. Both women and men at this conference should welcome the opportunity for dialogue that was given here, and

3. Both conferences on development and development projects, programs and policies should incorporate women and their concerns through inclusion of women in all stages of the planning cycle."

Manifesto for Development Now

(Prepared in concluding sessions and signed by 36 conference participants; later published in *New Maritimes* 3, no. 4 [December 1984–January 1985]:4)

"For over one hundred years much of what has come to be called 'development' in Atlantic Canada has been of such consequence that many people have been forced to leave this area while those remaining are and have been subject to the ravages of chronic unemployment and poor wages. Since the second world war many efforts have been made on behalf of the region to bring it up to the Canadian average and these efforts have been made in the name of regional development.

We, participants in this Conference, 'Rethinking Development in the 1980s,' deplore both the kind of efforts made and their inevitable consequence. We call for a different understanding of the whole development process and would call attention to certain features of our position in Atlantic Canada that lead us to an alternative, sustainable and equitable development. Development must include the following:

1. Female and male workers in Atlantic Canada must have more control over their present work environment with our goal being that eventually people will manage themselves in the world to such an extent that many will choose the type of work.
2. The appropriate way for workers to achieve a greater voice in their own development must be seen through their participation in unions, cooperatives and communities.
3. We cannot consider real democratic participation in development without outlining a real expansion in the role of women in community leadership and equality in the workplace.
4. The resources of the region are ours and that means that community control over development is the preferred option for defining what kind of development we want or will accept and how we will achieve its goals.
5. Notwithstanding the priority local communities must have respecting control over the pace and nature of development, we realize that history, population size, and prejudice have conspired to exclude many from sharing in our common resources and employment. Real development admits to all Atlantic Canadians regardless of race, ethnicity and gender.

Community control that is insensitive to women or to the position of any minority is a tyranny of the majority. Local communities must have effective control over the pace and nature of development.

6. Development links the people of this region with people throughout the world. They too must succeed in their efforts that we desire for ourselves. We wish the same amount of community control over local resources, the same participation of women in creating a truly developed society, and the same tolerance for minority positions that minorities accord the majority. We urge all to see development as 'our struggle' and we urge all to see equality as the true test of development efforts.

7. It is important to note, and we give this great emphasis—many of our present attempts at so-called development are little else but systematic rejections of citizens' participation in their own destiny and a desire by others to participate in the wealth we ourselves create.

8. Finally, we thank the people of Canada and the people of Nova Scotia for granting this forum for discussion on what must be done to rethink and eventually implement real development for all men, women and children."

Technology, Industrial Development, and Trade

Remarks by Anthony Winson

Our forum reminded me of salad dressing. Those of you who have prepared salad dressing know that oil and vinegar, if you don't do anything to them in the bowl, don't mix. What you need is a lot of shaking, and I must thank our chairperson, Ralph Henry, for providing the shaking. We got a mix somehow, and this is what we got:

First of all, technology, trade and development must meet human goals. Here we saw a need to stress community development, entrepreneurship and management. We believe that a commitment to enterprise must be fostered by a real control over the enterprise by those who are involved in it. There's a need for a holistic work environment, to make work more than strictly a means to an end. The idea is to give a responsibility to all employees.

We felt there was a need for an inventory of all development resources available, whether they be co-operative, entrepreneurial or state resources or whatever. And finally there was one phrase of one of the participants that really stuck in my mind and perhaps it could sum the thing up. Basically it was: Pieces of the structure furthest from the centre are the closest to the solution.

The Christian Church and Development

Remarks by Chairperson Gary Webster

I am going to report only about the Christian Church and development, although the Church is a non-governmental organization. It will be difficult to summarize the very productive forum we had as concisely as the other speakers have summarized theirs.

There was a concern on the part of the participants that a report to this plenary should reflect some of the concrete discussions of real circumstances that took place during the meeting, as opposed to simply putting forth a series of abstract propositions which we could all agree to, and we had no trouble agreeing to a number of abstract propositions.

First and foremost, the workshop emphasized that the Church has always played a role in development in the Caribbean and in other parts of the world, but that in earlier history the Church's role in development had been subordinate to the Church's conception of itself as an evangelizer. The task for the Church, both in Canada and in the Caribbean at this point, seems to be to elevate the role of the Church as concerned with human development, or development with a human face, to its properly integral position in faith and in the actualization of faith in human praxis.

It was emphasized that in all Christian traditions, regardless of their current institutional manifestations, the pursuit of justice is not an option. The scriptures necessarily imply a commitment to justice and the creation of a kingdom of justice in this world, not simply something pie in the sky by and by. The misinterpretations to which scripture has been subjected need to be challenged continually, both within individual denominations and on an ecumenical basis.

It was recognized that any commitment of the churches to development with justice must be carried out in an ecumenical framework, within a perspective of dialogue, with an intent to speak to people who are already professing Christians to work with people who are professing Christians, and to speak with those of other faiths and those of no faith.

There was a strong recognition on the part of all participants in the workshop that the Church must be where the people are, and when the Church (or the churches) wander from its (their) vocation, the people can continually remind them of the necessary justice and developmental components of the Christian faith; and thus you find the churches drawn back to their original vocation by the increasing visibility, audibility and actual progress within the so-called Third World. The Third World has, we recognize, called back the churches—the Catholic Church very obviously, for example—to their original commitment to development for all peoples, development with justice and equality.

I could go on at some length about concerns. We expressed concern about the role of the churches vis-à-vis corporations. There are innumerable interchurch task forces within Canada, for example, that preoccupy themselves with justice concerns. One of them is the Task Force on Churches and Corporate Responsibility (TCCR). The question of whether the churches should divest themselves of their shares in firms that trade with or do business in South Africa, that exploit the resources of Namibia or are involved in Chile, for example, was discussed and it is recognized that the churches are still wrestling with the most appropriate way to manifest their concern for justice in their relationships with corporations. Internally the churches certainly must complete a dialogue between those who currently understand the contradiction between investment in multinationals and the commitment to justice from a Christian perspective, and those who do not. And that dialogue must be ongoing.

Throughout our meeting we had a sense of commitment amongst all present to the realization that the current profound differences amongst Christians of different orientations and different institutional perspectives about just exactly what relationship churches have with development was bound to be present in this world. For example, the contradictions between the message of Jerry Falwell and the message of liberation theologians were simply something we were going to have to wrestle with in the faith, or at least the hope, that even Jerry Falwell may some day be converted to the original message of the scriptures. He may be born again, along with some other compatriots.

To sum up a few other themes quite quickly: The theme of participation in development was emphasized, the focus of the interchurch, 10-day, For World Development program for 1985, the perspective that there is no development without the full participation of all the peoples and all sectors amongst the peoples, particularly the most suppressed and exploited. Obviously, women, racial minorities, the unemployed and so on are required in this Christian vision of development with justice, not just to be marginal participants but to be seen as the source of truth, the source of redemption in this world.

I will at this point turn to the five propositions that Michael Clow formulated on our behalf:

"First, a purely pietistic understanding of Christianity is a limited guide to the search for moral values and moral actions in practical life.

Secondly, there is a need for the Christian churches to continue their promotion of a moral vision of development, with a primary focus on the meeting of human needs and on the critique of existing models and social theories of development.

Thirdly, the Church in the Caribbean and the Church in Canada face similar challenges to confront the reality and prospects of social, political and economic change.

Fourthly, Christian churches must contribute towards the construction of a future that reflects the vision of a kingdom of justice containing material adequacy or sufficiency for all.

Fifthly, the responsibility of Christians includes a practical concern with questions of justice and material development of all people."

I could add, sixthly, the concern that the churches maintain an ongoing dialogue from an ecumenical perspective amongst themselves, and with those who are not professing Christians.

Closing Remarks: A.A. MacDonald

(A.A. MacDonald is the Director of the Coady Institute at St. Francis Xavier University, Antigonish, Nova Scotia)

My pleasant task here is simply to close the conference by thanking those who organized it.

Let me say that I saw the purpose of this conference as one of arriving at a definition of development which would achieve a more humane more, as Jean Augustine put it today. Our methodology was one of workshops, plenary sessions and team speakers. I want to emphasize that I think the conference included a good cross section of people, both from the Atlantic region and from the Caribbean region, and I think we should acknowledge the effectiveness of the organizers in achieving that end.

I think another significant point is that we in the Atlantic region were exposed to some of the best-known Caribbean personalities—Manley, Moore, Jagan and others—and for that we in the Atlantic region are grateful to the Caribbean people who came here and participated in this conference with us.

I think the main thing was the sharing that took place. I think potential linkages have been established. I know that has been a result in my own case, and I hope that friendships have developed which will survive the differences of culture and ideology.

Appendices

Appendix 1: Conference Sponsors

The conference organizers acknowledge with appreciation the financial sponsorship and support of the following:

Canadian International Development Agency
Social Sciences and Humanities Research Council of Canada
Council of Maritime Premiers
Nova Scotia Departments of Development and Education
Canadian Association of Latin American and Caribbean Studies
Saint Mary's University
Institute for International Relations, University of the West Indies, St. Augustine, Trinidad
International Education Centre, Saint Mary's University
Gorsebrook Institute for Atlantic Canada Studies, Saint Mary's University
International Development Studies, Saint Mary's University
Atlantic Provinces Economic Council, Halifax.

Appendix 2: Conference Program

Thursday, October 25

4:00-8:00 pm   Registration

5:30-7:30 pm   Reception

8:00 pm   **Opening Addresses**

Speaker: Robert Moore (Past High Commissioner
of Guyana to Canada)

"From the 1960s to the 1980s"

Speaker: Rev. Dale Bisnauth (Caribbean Council of
Churches; Ecumenical Council of Canada)

*"Canada and the Caribbean: Re-examining an
Important Relationship"*

Chair: George Schuyler (International Education
Centre, Saint Mary's)

Friday, October 26   Plenary Sessions

8:30 am   Continental Breakfast

9:00-12:00 pm   DEVELOPMENT MODELS AND THEORIES: AN
ASSESSMENT

Kari Levitt (McGill)
Cheddi Jagan, M.P. (Leader of the Opposition, Guyana)
James Sacouman (Acadia)

Discussant: Miguel Murmis (University of Toronto)

Chair: Anthony Winson (Gorsebrook Institute for
Atlantic Canada Studies, Saint Mary's)

12:15-1:15 pm   Lunch

1:25-1:30 pm   Civic Welcome by Mayor of Halifax Ron Wallace

1:30-4:30 pm   REGIONAL DEVELOPMENT: ISSUES AND
                RESOURCES

                Herb Addo (IIR, Trinidad)
                Ramesh Ramsaran (IIR, Trinidad)
                Dan MacInnes (St. Francis Xavier)
                Tom Kent (Dalhousie)
                Benjamin Higgins (University of the South Pacific)

                Chair: Rudophe Lamarche (Institut Canadien de
                    Reserche sur le Developpement Regional, Moncton)

7:00-9:00 pm   Banquet hosted by Nova Scotia Department of
                Development

                Speaker: Robert Moore (Past High Commissioner of
                    Guyana to Canada)

                "Canada and the Caribbean in a World of Crises"

                Chair: George Schuyler (International Education
                    Centre, Saint Mary's)

9:00-1:00 am   Caribbean Dance and Entertainment

Saturday, October 27   Workshop Sessions

8:30 am   Continental Breakfast

9:00-10:45 am   ROLE OF THE STATE IN DEVELOPMENT

                James Petras (State University of New York,
                    Binghamton)
                Rick Williams (Dalhousie)
                Peter Phillips (U.W.I., Mona)
                Gary Webster (University of P.E.I.)

                Discussant: Michael Kaufman (York University)

                Chair: Colin Leys (Queen's University at Kingston)

MODELS OF AGRICULTURAL DEVELOPMENT

Argelia Tejada (Research Institute of the Dominican
    Republic; National University)
Anthony Winson (Gorsebrook Institute, Saint Mary's)

Discussant: J.T.G. Andrew (Deputy Minister of
    Agriculture, N.B.)

Chair: Bob Thompson (Agriculture Canada; Ontario
    Public Interest Research Group)

WOMEN AND DEVELOPMENT

Peggy Antrobus (U.W.I., Cave Hill, Barbados)
Anne Bishop (CUSO)
Jean Stubbs (Havana)
Lynette Mensah (Dalhousie)

Chair: Mary Turner (Dalhousie)

FINANCE AND AID IN DEVELOPMENT

Cheddi Jagan (Leader of the Opposition, Guyana)
Michael Bradfield (Dalhousie)
William Demas (Caribbean Development Bank,
    Barbados)
Anthony Gonzales (IIR, Trinidad)

Chair: Amon Niko (Dalhousie)

EMPLOYMENT AND UNEMPLOYMENT

David Abdulla (Oil Field Workers Trade Union,
    Trinidad and Tobago)
Richard Cashin (Newfoundland Fishermen, Food and
    Allied Workers Union)
Farley S. Brathwaite (U.W.I., Cave Hill)
Robert Hill (Memorial)

Chair: John Harker (CLC)

INDUSTRIALIZATION AS DEVELOPMENT

Ramesh Ramsaran (IIR, Trinidad)
Ivor Harrington (N.S. Dept. of Development)
Pinar Bulca (Technical University of Nova Scotia)

Chair: John Chamard (Saint Mary's)

11:00-12:45 pm INDUSTRIALIZATION AS DEVELOPMENT:
MEGAPROJECTS

Ralph Henry (U.W.I., St. Augustine)
James Bickerton (St. Francis Xavier)
Andrew Secord (Saint Mary's; Saint Thomas)

Chair: Michael Clow (Saint Mary's)

RACE AND CLASS, LABOUR AND MIGRATON

Rosina Wiltshire-Brodber (IIR, Trinidad)
Gail R. Pool (University of New Brunswick)
Cheddi Jagan (Leader of the Opposition, Guyana)
Dorothy Moore (Dalhousie)

Chair: Tony Johnstone (N.S. Dept. of Education)

ORGANIZING PRIMARY PRODUCERS

Michael Belliveau (Maritime Fishermen's Union, N.S.)
Peter deMarsh (N.B. Woodlot Owners Association)
Marie Burge (National Farmers Union, P.E.I.)
David Abdulla (Oil Field Workers Trade Union,
    Trinidad and Tobago)

Chair: Rick Williams (Dalhousie)

COMMUNITY DEVELOPMENT AND
REVITALIZATION

Michael Witter (U.W.I., Mona)
Neville Duncan (U.W.I., Cave Hill)
Tim O'Neill (Saint Mary's)
A.A. MacDonald (Coady Institute, St. Francis Xavier)

Discussant: Greg Allain (Université de Moncton)

Chair: Ron Ryan (Community Developer, Guysborough, N.S.)

CARIBBEAN–ATLANTIC CANADA TRADE

Milan Solarik (External Affairs Canada)
Louis Wiltshire (CARICOM, Guyana)
Ron McDonough (N.B. Dept. of Commerce and Development)
Phil Thompson (Writer; ACCESS)

Discussant: Desmond Thomas (McGill)

Chair: Harvey Silverstein (Maritime Technology Consultants)

12:45-2:00 pm   Luncheon hosted by the Council of Maritime Premiers

Speaker: Louis Wiltshire (CARICOM)

"CARICOM and Regional Co-operation in the Caribbean"

Chair: Colin Howell (Gorsebrook Institute, Saint Mary's)

2:00-4:00 pm   MODELS OF FISHERIES DEVELOPMENT

Lennox Hinds (CIDA)
Peter Sinclair (Memorial)
Orestes Gonzales Caballero (Ministry of Fisheries, Cuba)
Svein Jentoft (University of Tromso)

Chair: Gene Barrett (Saint Mary's)

TECHNOLOGY AND MANAGEMENT IN DEVELOPMENT

Jacqueline Archer (Caribbean Industrial Research Institute, Trinidad)
Yassin Sankar (Dalhousie)
Harvey Silverstein (Maritime Technology Consultants)
Tom Nickerson (N.S. Research Foundation Corp.)

Chair: Phil Thompson (Writer; ACCESS)

ROLE OF NGOs IN DEVELOPMENT

Oscar Allen (St. Vincent, U.W.I.)
Joan Campbell (Development and Peace, Halifax)
Marlene Greene (CUSO, Ottawa)
Bob Thompson (Ontario Public Interest Research Group)

Chair: George Schuyler (International Education Centre, Saint Mary's)

ORGANIZING FOR CHANGE

Barry Chevannes (U.W.I., Mona)
Gilles Theriault (Maritime Fishermen's Union, Shediac)
David Abdulla (Oil Field Workers Trade Union, Trinidad and Tobago)
Alexa McDonough (Leader, N.S. New Democratic Party)

Chair: James Sacouman (Acadia University)

LEGAL ISSUES AND DIPLOMACY IN
DEVELOPMENT

Anthony Bryan (IIR, Trinidad)
Anselm Francis (IIR, Trinidad)
Elizabeth Mann Borgese (Dalhousie)

Chair: Tom Donovan (Crossroads International,
Halifax)

4:00-5:15 pm   **Summation Address**

James Petras (State University of New York,
Binghamton)

"Development in the 1980s and Beyond"

5:30-7:00 pm   Dinner

7:00-9:00 pm   Speaker: Michael Manley, M.P. (Former Prime
Minister of Jamaica)

*"Caribbean Development in Historical
Perspective"*

9:00-12:00 pm   Reception and Dance

Sunday, October 28

10:00 am   Continental Breakfast

10:30-11:30 am LOCAL GOVERNMENT INITIATIVES

Ron McDonough (N.B. Dept. of Commerce and
Development)
Ralph Henry (U.W.I., St. Augustine)
Jacqueline Archer (Caribbean Industrial Research
Institute, Trinidad)

Chair: George Schuyler (International Education
Centre, Saint Mary's)

11:30-12:30 am   Lunch

>Speaker: Jean Augustine (Canadian Advisory Council on the Status of Women; Congress of Black Women in Canada)

>*"Third World Canadians and the Question of Development"*

>Chair: Colin Howell (Gorsebrook Institute, Saint Mary's)

1:00-3:00 pm   **Open Forums**

>Rethinking Development (Chair: James Petras)

>Women and Development (Chair: Jean Augustine)

>Development Education (Chair: Robert Moore)

>Technology, Industrial Development, and Trade (Chair: Ralph Henry)

>The Christian Church and Development (Chair: Gary Webster)

3:00 pm   Closing Remarks: A.A. MacDonald

Appendix 3: Program Participants

David Abdulla, Secretary-Treasurer, Oil Field Workers Trade Union of Trinidad and Tobago

Herb Addo, Institute of International Relations, St. Augustine, Trinidad

Greg Allain, Sociology, Université de Moncton, New Brunswick

Oscar Allen, Director, Projects Promotion, St. Vincent, University of the West Indies

J.T.G. Andrew, Deputy Minister of Agriculture, New Brunswick

Peggy Antrobus, Extra Mural Studies, Women and Development, University of the West Indies, Cave Hill, Barbados

Jacqueline Archer, Information Specialist, Caribbean Industrial Research Institute, Trinidad

Jean Augustine, Canadian Advisory Council on the Status of Women, Congress of Black Women of Canada

Gene Barrett, Sociology, Saint Mary's University, Halifax

Elizabeth Beale, Chief Economist, Atlantic Provinces Economic Council, Halifax

Michael Belliveau, Maritime Fishermen's Union, Nova Scotia

James Bickerton, Political Science, St. Francis Xavier University, Antigonish, Nova Scotia

Anne Bishop, Canadian University Service Overseas

Dale Bisnauth, Caribbean Council of Churches, Ecumenical Council of Canada

Elizabeth Mann Borgese, International Ocean Affairs, Dalhousie University, Halifax

Michael Bradfield, Economics, Dalhousie University, Halifax

Farley S. Brathwaite, Social Science, University of the West Indies, Cave Hill, Barbados

Anthony Bryan, Director, Institute of International Relations, St. Augustine, Trinidad

Pinar Bulca, Urban Planning, Technical University of Nova Scotia, Halifax

Marie Burge, National Farmers Union, Prince Edward Island

Orestes Gonzales Caballero, Head, Department of Scientific and Technical Information, Ministry of Fisheries, Havana, Cuba

Joan Campbell, Director, Development and Peace, Halifax

Richard Cashin, President, Newfoundland Fishermen, Food and Allied Workers Union, St. John's

John Chamard, Management, Saint Mary's University, Halifax

Barry Chevannes, Anthropology, University of the West Indies, Mona, Jamaica; Worker's Party

Michael Clow, Sociology, Saint Mary's University, Halifax
Peter deMarsh, President, New Brunswick Woodlot Owners Association
William Demas, President, Caribbean Development Bank, Barbados
Tom Donovan, Director, Crossroads International, Halifax
Emery Fanjoy, Secretary, Council of Maritime Premiers
Anthony Gonzales, Institute of International Relations, St. Augustine, Trinidad
Marlene Greene, Canadian University Service Overseas, Ottawa
John Groves, Director of Trade and Tourism, Department of Regional Industrial Expansion, Canada
John Harker, Director, International Affairs, Caribbean Desk, Canadian Labour Congress, Toronto, Ontario
Ivor Harrington, Department of Development, Nova Scotia
Ralph Henry, Economics, University of the West Indies, St. Augustine, Trinidad
Benjamin Higgins, Director, Centre for Applied Studies in Development, University of the South Pacific
Robert Hill, Sociology, Memorial University, St. John's, Newfoundland
Lennox Hinds, Caribbean Fisheries Specialist, Canadian International Development Agency
Cheddi Jagan, Leader of the Opposition, Guyana
Svein Jentoft, Institute of Fisheries, University of Tromso, Norway
Tony Johnstone, Co-ordinator of Ethnic Services, Department of Education, Nova Scotia
Michael Kaufman, Political Science, York University, Downsview, Ontario
Tom Kent, Public Administration, Dalhousie University, Halifax
Rudolph Lamarche, Research Co-ordinator, Institut Canadien de Reserche sur le Developpement Regional, Moncton, New Brunswick
Kari Levitt, Centre for Developing Area Studies, McGill University, Montreal
Colin Leys, Political Studies, Queen's University at Kingston
A.A. MacDonald, Director, Coady Institute, St. Francix Xavier University, Antigonish, Nova Scotia
Dan MacInnes, Coady Institute, St. Francis Xavier University, Antigonish, Nova Scotia
Peter MacLellan, Atlantic Canada Studies, Saint Mary's University, Halifax
Michael Manley, Member of Parliament, Former Prime Minister of Jamaica
Ian McAllister, Director, Centre for Development Projects, Dalhousie University, Halifax
Alexa McDonough, Leader, Nova Scotia New Democratic Party

Ron McDonough, Policy Planner, New Brunswick Department of Commerce and Development
Hugh Mellon, Atlantic Canada Studies, Saint Mary's University, Halifax
Lynette Mensah, Nursing, Dalhousie University, Halifax
Frances Michel, President, Farm Workers Union; People's Labour Party, St. Lucia
Dorothy Moore, Maritime School of Social Work, Dalhousie University, Halifax
Robert Moore, Past High Commissioner of Guyana to Canada
Miguel Murmis, Sociology, University of Toronto
Tom Nickerson, Nova Scotia Research Foundation Corporation, Dartmouth, Nova Scotia
Amon Niko, Senior Fellow, Development Projects, Dalhousie University, Halifax
Brian O'Neill, Oxfam, Halifax
Tim O'Neill, Economics, Saint Mary's University, Halifax
James Petras, Sociology, State University of New York, Binghamton
Peter Phillips, Government and Sociology, University of the West Indies, Mona, Jamaica
Gail R. Pool, Anthropology, University of New Brunswick, Fredericton
Ramesh Ramsaran, Senior Advisor, International Economic Relations, Institute of International Relations, St. Augustine, Trinidad
Ron Ryan, Community Developer, Guysborough, Nova Scotia
James Sacouman, Sociology, Acadia University, Wolfville, Nova Scotia
Yassin Sankar, Management, Dalhousie University, Halifax
George Schuyler, Director, International Education Centre, Saint Mary's University, Halifax
Andrew Secord, Economics, Saint Mary's University, Halifax; St. Thomas University, Fredericton, New Brunswick
Harvey Silverstein, President, Maritime Technology Consultants Ltd., Halifax
Peter Sinclair, Sociology, Memorial University, St. John's, Newfoundland
Keith Lyn Smith, Head of Trade Union Congress, Antigua
Michael Smith, Atlantic Canada Studies, Saint Mary's University, Halifax
Milan Solarik, Director, Trade and Development for Caribbean and Central America, External Affairs Canada
Bob Stuart, President, Atlantic Provinces Economic Council, Halifax
Jean Stubbs, Labour Historian, Havana, Cuba
Argelia Tejada, President, Research Institute for the Dominican Republic; Sociology, Pedro Henriquez Urena, National University, Santo Domingo

Gilles Theriault, President, Maritime Fishermen's Union, Shediac, New Brunswick

Desmond Thomas, Centre for Developing Area Studies, McGill University, Montreal

Bob Thompson, Agriculture Canada; Ontario Public Interest Research Group

Phil Thompson, Writer specializing in community development and energy; Co-ordinator of the Atlantic Canada Community Energy Strategy Society (ACCESS)

Mary Turner, History, Dalhousie University, Halifax

Henry Veltmeyer, Sociology, Saint Mary's University, Halifax

Gary Webster, Political Science, University of Prince Edward Island, Charlottetown

Terrance White, Atlantic Canada Studies, Saint Mary's University, Halifax

Rick Williams, Maritime School of Social Work, Dalhousie University, Halifax

Louis Wiltshire, Deputy Director, CARICOM, Guyana

Rosina Wiltshire-Brodber, Institute of International Relations, St. Augustine, Trinidad

Anthony Winson, Director, Gorsebrook Institute for Atlantic Canada Studies, Saint Mary's University, Halifax

Michael Witter, Economics, University of the West Indies, Mona, Jamaica